Working with Children and Parents

Working with Children and Parents

Edited by
Kirkland C. Vaughans, Ph.D.

Routledge
Taylor & Francis Group
New York London

First published by Other Press LLC

This edition published 2012 by Routledge

Routledge
Taylor & Francis Group
711 Third Avenue
New York, NY 10017

Routledge
Taylor & Francis Group
27 Church Road, Hove
East Sussex BN3 2FA

Production Editor: Robert D. Hack

ISBN 978-0-881-63802-8

Table of Contents

JicaP Vol. 2, No. 2, 2002

Trends in Child Development and the Family

Judith Wallerstein, Ph.D.

Author's Note

I was invited to address the Chief Justices of the United States at their Annual Meeting on August 1, 2000, in Rapid City, South Dakota. The theme of my talk was to be "Trends in Child Development and the Family." The National Council of Juvenile and Family Courts wished me to cover the following topics in the hour and a half that I was allotted: attachment theory, the impact of separation and loss on the child, the trauma of removal, the child's concept of time, and issues of witnessing domestic violence. At first, I was alarmed and amused by the magnitude of the assignment and the meagerness of the time frame, but I soon realized that the Council members had no idea about the complexity of the issues they wanted addressed, and that, in fact, their expectations reflected the state of their understanding of psychological issues. I was assured that they would have no objection to my selecting from among the subjects suggested and setting my own priorities as to which were the most urgent.

I also discovered that I was the only non-legal professional on the program, and that I would be preceded by U.S. Supreme Court Justice Sandra Day O'Connor and followed by several judges who deal primarily with dependent children and issues of child welfare.

I embarked on several lines of inquiry in making my choice of subjects and preparing my presentation. First, I approached several child research colleagues, among them Steve Seligman and Alicia Lieberman, to make sure that I was up to date on the latest research findings in attachment. I also called Judge Edwards of the Santa Clara Court in California, who was slated to follow my presentation, to discuss his agenda so that my talk might align with his interest in obtaining increased family court resources from within the legal system in California. I then spoke with a number of practicing attorneys, law professors, and Appellate Court judges to find out what I might expect in the way of understanding and response to my ideas from the Chief Justices. And I interviewed several members of CASA (Court Appointed Special Advocates), a lay organization that does intensive volunteer work with children in the child welfare system and the family courts, to find out what is really happening to these children, and how policies are implemented, or not implemented, by the courts and the various official groups that are assigned by the courts to carry out these tasks.

I thought long and hard about what approach I could use that would best engage my audience. I had learned that in all probability none of the Chief Justices I would be addressing had ever sat on a family court bench or been involved in any way with family or children's issues. I assumed from my past experience in speaking with judges, and from the advice of people I had consulted, that I might well expect them to be bored or put off by any sort of statistical, or technical, or pontifical presentation, or by one that dealt with sweeping generalities. Accordingly, I began with a dramatic approach that I hoped would arouse their interest and mark my talk as different from what they expected. I relied on real-life examples drawn from current family court cases to raise hard questions that I hoped they would find challenging and troubling. I said very little in praise of current court practices and did not refrain from criticizing judges or policies that have failed to protect children. I tried to explain psychological concepts like *attachment* and *cognitive development* in everyday terms that would be "user friendly." My initial concern was to level the playing field between us and to approach my audience as colleagues, without the deference and ceremony to which they are accustomed.

In my opening remarks, I bypassed their official roles as Chief Justices and reached out to them as parents and grandparents. In brief, I first tried to touch them emotionally, in order, then, to impress them intellectually with my very serious message that our advancing knowledge enables us—indeed, requires us—to reach a clearer and quicker understanding of children and parents in family crisis situations, and, most importantly, to impress upon them that the courts hold the lives of thousands of children in the balance without having the requisite training or resources to serve them justly.

From the long applause and the many questions that followed my presentation, as well as from later discussions and correspondence with several of the Chief Justices, my overall sense is that I succeeded in grasping the attention of my audience, that they listened carefully, and that a number of them were moved by the urgency of the task before us.

* * * * * *

I have been asked to talk with you about recent advances in child development and the family. The suggested agenda, which I received from the National Council of Juvenile and Family Courts, includes attachment theory, the impact of separation and loss on the child, the trauma of removal, the child's concept of time, and issues of witnessing domestic violence. I would like as well to note some of the pressing problems that children, parents, and the courts confront during and after divorce.

Because our time together is short, and I need to build a bridge this afternoon between the world of the child and the world of the courts so that we can understand each other, I ask that you bring to mind a child you know and love, preferably a young child, your own child, or a grandchild, perhaps a great-grandchild. I suggest a young child because the children whose lives we address in the courts today are young and getting younger. Half of the one million children who experience their parents' divorce yearly are 6 years old or below. Forty percent of the half million in the child welfare system were 6 or younger at the time of their first contact with the legal system. The numbers of both groups cluster significantly within the first three years of life. Our responsibility is to these vulnerable children, during their most vulnerable years, when the potential for lasting disruption to their development poses its greatest threat. As the record shows—and as the jury of children who have grown to adulthood after divorce or after graduating from the child welfare system tell us—we have not served them well on our watch.

There has been in the past two decades an explosion in our knowledge about children and how they grow, knowledge that has transformed our understanding of human development. The explosion comes out of dazzling research into the brain; remarkable new techniques that enable us to observe the infant during the first few days and weeks of life; studies of the cognitive, social, and moral development of children; research about children who witness violence, children in high-conflict divorces, and in joint and sole custody; as well as long-term studies that follow children well into adult life and reveal the long-lasting influence of early parent–child relationships—of both good and poor parenting—and the intergenerational transmission of the effects of childhood trauma, parental divorce, and the experience of violence in the home.

As the result of this explosion in our knowledge, there is a wide and growing gulf between what we have learned and the thinking that undergirds policies and practices in the courts. There is hardly any preparatory or ongoing provision within the legal system for educating judges and court personnel regarding children or family relationships, or for keeping judges apprised of important research advances as they occur. As a result, neither judges nor parents nor children benefit from what we know. Judges today are emotionally overtaxed and intellectually baffled by the questions before them in which the legal issues may not be the decisive or most important factor. They lack a frame of reference for thinking about—let alone deciding—whether a child of 3 weeks, 3 months, or 3 years should be court-ordered to spend consecutive days and overnights in the father's home, and whether or when to trust or to override the mother's anxiety about separating from her child. Or—to refer to a case in recent memory of a 12-year-old who was literally ordered shackled and detained when she refused to visit her father, whose moral values she abhorred and rejected—for answering the defining question: Was that child right in her admonition to the Illinois judge: "You are making the greatest mistake of your life"?

What will be the lasting effect of that judge's order? Will the child, as a result of her encounter with the legal system, be motivated to study law in order to become, herself, a more compassionate judge? Or will she turn her back bitterly on the adult society that she feels betrayed her? How important is it for the court, when it deals with children, to assess not only the legal issues but also the impact of the court order on the developing child, and in this instance, and others, the moral sensibility of the child? And how shall the court do that?

Should a child who has witnessed intermittent violence between her parents be removed and placed with strangers in a shelter or a foster family? When should the court leave bad-enough alone, because the hazards of child removal outweigh the hazards of the child's remaining in the family? And how can the judge make that decision without a frame of reference that includes an understanding of the developing child and the effects on her of witnessing violence? Or, finally, when it is reasonable for the judge to order two parents, who are yoked together in high conflict and rage, to provide two good-enough homes for the child in a joint physical custody arrangement? When do such orders serve to increase the child's suffering and place the child in greater psychological jeopardy? All of these questions, which judges address daily, require decisions that draw only in part on their legal background and training.

I will try today to provide a framework for considering some of the major issues that courts address, in the light of what we know about children and families. My purpose is not to propose a degree in psychology for already overburdened judges, but rather to paint in broad strokes the background information they require in order to ease their tasks and enable the court in good conscience to safeguard the interests of the child.

I turn first to attachment, which is the dominant paradigm in our understanding of how infants and young children begin their life journey, and how and why they fail. Relationships are central to our lives. We know that intuitively. We have learned only recently, however, that babies come into the world prepared for relationships with others. The human child is helpless at birth. Of all the animal species, the human child has no capacity to survive alone. He cannot protect himself from predators or provide in any way for his own needs, even in the minimal ways that newborns in other species come better equipped to do. Moreover, his helplessness, without an adult lifeline, lasts for many, many years. As soon as he learns to crawl, he crawls into the fireplace. As soon as he can walk, he walks out the sixth floor window. But the human race has survived because, as it turns out, the human child comes into the world with a powerful capacity to evoke a response for care. He can cry; and that cry arouses room service around the clock—changing, rocking, cuddling, walking the floor all night: "Don't cry baby, please don't cry," say the frantic parents whom he has just met.

We used to think of the human baby as passive. Nothing could be further from the truth. He comes ready to engage. His eyes apparently focus at 8 to 12 inches, exactly the distance between the breast and the mother's face. And he can recognize his mother, by voice, by smell, by whatever, within a few days after delivery. Mostly, he comes into the world programmed to stay close to the primary caregiver, usually the mother. And in the first year of life, child and mother create a biologically based, passionate relationship. The roots of this relationship, which we call attachment, are the survival of the helpless child and the behaviors of the child that increase the child–mother proximity and thereby increase the protective and survival chances of the child. Attachment is a characteristic of humans throughout their life span. It is not an immature behavior that we need to outgrow. Everyone of us here has, at every age, at least one person whom we want nearby when we are frightened or in pain.

Attachment is specific. Attachment figures are not at all interchangeable. Your mother, your wife, your daughter is not just any nearby lady. Many of the most intense feelings arise during the formation of the attachment relationship. It's like falling in love. Threats of loss arouse anxiety. Loss gives way to deep mourning. Why is this relationship so important? Because the attachment relationship is central to the child's entire development. It is the axis around which the child's development grows. The child's view of himself, of the attachment parent, of the entire world, is largely based on the availability of that attachment figure. The judge must learn to factor in the child's attachment when he considers changing custody or moving a child into adoption or joint custody. Parents who are equal in law, like mother and father, or equal in parenting skills, may not be equal in the child's attachment schema. High or low self-esteem begins exactly here. A child who feels secure in the availability and protection of her mother feels that she is a good child; after all, Mother takes care of her. Mother and Father and the whole family applaud her first step, her first words. She feels herself to be a competent child, who can make things happen: "I cry, and she comes running." She feels like a lovable person because she is indeed loved and protected. She learns very soon to treat herself the way she is treated, and this becomes the basis for a lifelong self-image.

The opposite is all too familiar to those of us who work with troubled children in the court system and elsewhere. "I'm not lovable," thinks the child. "She scowls at me, and hits me." "I'm powerless," he thinks. "I lie in the crib all day and cry and cry, and no one comes. I'm hungry, and no one feeds. I'm a bad child, a horrid child, a castaway whom no one wants."

Of course, later life experiences are important. But at rock bottom are the attachments of infancy and the early childhood years, between primary caregiver and child. To feel secure, to feel safe and protected, is the greatest gift in the world. Such lucky children are likely, according to our studies, to have good relationships with their peers, to learn better, to expect people to treat them decently and well, to get along with teachers, to get along in the world. A secure child can learn well because he is able to take off from a secure base to explore, first the nursery, then the playground, then the greater world, knowing that he has a lap that will be there if he falls and a parent who will kiss him and make it well if he gets hurt. He has mastered the first rung of the developmental ladder that extends throughout life: he has learned to trust.

Attachment theory explains the significance of separation and rejection for the child. It offers a compelling explanation for the overwhelming anxiety associated with the trauma of separation and loss, for the fear, the anxiety, the anger and the sadness, when the child's lifeline of safety is disrupted.

Infants and children in reasonably good or adequate families are able to form more than one attachment. These can be to the biological parents, to older siblings, to grandparents, to other members of the household. Children form attachments to their fathers even when they see them infrequently. There may be a special quality to that relationship that the child responds to. But the number of attachments is by no means limitless, and it is important to realize that children with several attachments have an attachment hierarchy. There is a strong tendency for infants and young children to prefer one principal figure for comfort and security, usually the mother.

Of course, as you have undoubtedly guessed, the children who are brought to the child welfare system rarely show secure attachments to their primary caregiver. On the contrary, they show a wide range from moderately insecure to disorganized attachment, and their behavior in the presence of that parent can range from avoiding contact altogether, to rejecting her in anger, to becoming disorganized in her presence. These partly or predominantly insecure attachments reflect the child's tragic sense of having been inadequately cared for and poorly protected. And a very insecure attachment, where the child becomes disorganized and jumps around at random, exhibiting anxiety when reunited with the caregiver, is associated with a wide range of psychopathology, including suicidal behaviors, substance abuse, delinquency in adolescence, and personality disorders in adult life. Insecurity in attachment is prominent in children exposed to physical abuse, neglect, institutional rearing, and high conflict.

What is particularly difficult for adults to understand is that, out of their intense need for survival and protection, children can and do become attached to adults who hurt them, to people who abuse them, to people who exploit them sexually, neglect and starve them, or threaten them in many ways. The human child's capacity to attach is not dependent on the caregiver's kindness. Rather, it reflects the child's need to feel the safety of familiarity, even with a bad person. Better any attachment, however painful, than being alone or with strangers. Paradoxically as well, children suffer as much from being separated from a bad attachment figure as they do from being separated from a loving parent. They have, after all, no reason whatsoever to assume that the would-be rescuer will treat them differently or better. In fact, they cling to the bad attachment figure because, hurtful as he is, he is the devil you know, and he is preferable to the unknown predators that circle out there. All separations from either secure or very insecure attachments are therefore followed by profound anxiety. The child is worried about her survival in a dangerous world.

In my new book, which records twenty-five years in the lives of one hundred children of divorce from childhood through full adulthood, I give the example of the intense attachment of a little boy, age 9, to his father who had hit him, beaten his mother, and mistreated his beloved sister. One day, as father and child drove past some high-voltage wires, the child asked, "Dad, how powerful are those lines?" The father made a guess about the voltage. "Dad," said the child, "I would grab those wires for you." "Dad," he said, "I would die for you." Stick with me, I need you, says the human child to the man who has hurt him more than anyone in the world. Perhaps from this you can infer the despair of these abused children or children who have witnessed parental violence.

Because children are attached to good and bad parents, the issue of whether to separate a child from her parents, or maintain her there, cannot be based on the passion of the child's attachment to the parent. We cannot conclude from the strength of the child's attachment whether the charges of abuse or neglect are well or ill founded. We need to know the nature of the attachment, what it is based on, and where it leads, in order to pass judgment. For example, a violent parent is often an admired and exciting figure for the child, as well as an object of terror. He is loved and hated simultaneously. And although the child may love and pity the victim, it is more exciting and safer for the child to identify with the aggressor. Such attachments with the aggressor are dangerous for the future development of the child. They can be powerful and long lasting, and they represent one of the dangers of being raised in a violent family.

Let me clarify the complex issues that go with separation and termination of a relationship. First, it is important to keep in mind that children will keep secret the abusive experiences within the family. In part, they do so out of fear of punishment and fear of being excluded by the parent or parents. These are realistic fears, in my experience. But additionally, it is important to understand that the child will do whatever is necessary, emotionally or any other way—he will grasp the high-voltage wire, or its equivalent in other domains of life—to maintain the attachment and to defend against the disruption of the relationship.

When you remove an adult from a dangerous situation and place that adult where she is safe from harm, you can feel good about the rescue, and you can relax and take sufficient time to make new plans for her future. When you remove a young child from a bad, bad situation, where the child is starving or filthy or bleeding, you can feel good about having rescued that child from physical harm, disease, or even death, but the child does not feel grateful. She does not feel rescued. She is terrified. She carries within her powerful, overwhelming technicolor images of her experience, and—make no mistake about it—she expects the same treatment from her rescuer, from all of us. This is the world as she knows it: Grown-ups are not necessarily kind and generous; they are capricious, cruel, and demanding. The frightened child comes into a shelter, where she may feel in greater danger than in her home. Moreover, not only is the child alone and frightened, and feeling abandoned by her family; what makes it even worse, the child feels that she is to blame; she is the wicked little girl who made a mess and is being driven away. When parents divorce, little children blame themselves. When parents hit them, little children feel that they are bad. When children are removed, they feel that they are being excluded from the family because they are evil. It's not until children reach 7 or 8 years of age that they begin to understand cause and effect as we adults think of it. Until then, the child's thinking is *me*-centered. If things go well, the child feels she is good; if things go badly, the child blames herself because it is far too frightening to blame the powerful parent, for then she would really have no protection, and no chance to survive in a dangerous world.

I cannot stress too strongly that the judge needs to understand that the child, after removal, and even if she is in a safe, warm place, is just as much in a state of emergency as when she was in her troubled home. She's terrified and guilty everywhere she looks. There is no real shelter for her, in the shelter or in the foster home, until she has a permanent place she can call home. She may make life very difficult for her rescuers until she gradually begins to believe that she has a safe place where she can stay. In an article by Judge Leonard Edwards, whom you will hear from shortly, which he published in 1997, he notes, in accord with these formulations, that judges and all other participants in the judicial abuse and neglect process should treat each case as if it were an emergency. He says, and I quote his words, "Children and families are in trauma. The longer the process takes, the more intensive their trauma."

A long time ago, Goldstein, Freud, and Solnit, in their classic books, told us, "You can't put a child on ice." Exactly. You can't keep a child in limbo. He needs a permanent place, whether he returns to his original home, or whether he can start again in a new, safer place. Selection of where the child will grow up needs to be made quickly, with the recognition that unless the child has a place with a sense of permanence and safety, where he can find an appropriate figure and reestablish his attachment needs, he will be severely handicapped emotionally and socially and in his ability to learn. You can't learn from teachers or adults whom you don't trust.

I am of course fully aware that the child's intense needs for speedy settlement often conflict with the parents' wishes and rights to employ a full range of adversarial strategies that are inherent in the judicial process. Nevertheless, these rights need to be balanced against the needs of the child who is in an emergency situation; when he has no permanent home and no attachment figure with him, the child is in great danger of losing his chance for a decent life, not only for the present but forever.

About fifteen years ago, I was asked by a major department of child welfare to give a series of lectures to their senior professional staff. I learned, to my astonishment, that they had a deliberate policy of not leaving the child in any foster home longer than three months so as to avoid the child's becoming attached to a family that presumably the child would leave, either to return to his own home or to go into a permanent placement. The presumption of the policy was that if they moved the child frequently, they would spare him the grief of loss, and that he would then be better able to adjust to a family when the final decisions were made about his placement. I cannot tell you how distressed I was at the cruelty and heartlessness of inflicting separation after separation upon the child. I said, "If your goal in this agency was to promote emptiness in relationships and promiscuity in these children, then you have succeeded admirably with this policy, and I congratulate you." I won't tell you the rest, but they were surely shaken.

Let me now present a more optimistic view. Let me take you with me to meet Lois, a 2-year-old child who was already showing some of these features of an empty, shallow relationship pattern, but this time we were able to reverse it. (This case is taken from the work of Professor Alicia Lieberman at the University of California in San Francisco.) Lois was referred for assessment because her adoptive parents were concerned that they had been unable to establish a relationship with her. They complained that she was friendly with everybody in the same way, and something about her wasn't "real." At 2 years! They wanted to know whether she would ever become attached to them, and whether she would ever love them. (Let me here interpolate that many adoptive homes break up because the child with a history of multiple placements and traumatic experiences is unresponsive, ungratifying, and heartbreaking to parents who want to love the child and be loved by her.) Lois had been raised by an emotionally unstable mother from birth until 6 months of age. During this period, she experienced many changes of caregivers, as the mother frequently dropped her off to stay with various relatives and friends. Although the friends were well meaning, they surely did not give the child priority in their lives. Lois was removed from the home by Child Protective Services after a neighbor reported that the mother had dropped off the child, presumably for three hours, and failed to return after three days. The child welfare workers described Lois as delightfully friendly, outgoing, eminently adoptable, a child who seldom cried. Actually, as we were soon to learn, it was a mask of affability—yes, 2-year-old children can wear masks—to protect herself against being hurt once again.

After removal from her biological mother, Lois stayed for three months in a shelter, after which she was transferred to a foster home. The adoptive home was found four months later, and a few months after that she was permanently placed there. Although the youngster was then 2 years old, she had already experienced three major changes in caregivers, in addition to the changes she experienced while she was living with her mother for the first six months of her life.

During our first meeting, which took place in her new home, Lois smiled all the time, as had been described by the adoptive mother. Within a few minutes, she made herself the center of attention, bringing a stuffed animal charmingly to the clinician, asking to look in her purse, running back and forth, and acting toward the adoptive mother the same way that she did with the psychologist whom she had just met. The women seemed clearly interchangeable to her. The adoptive mother said, "See what I mean? She'll go to anybody." During the second visit, held at the agency, the child walked into office after office on her way to the playroom, without checking back with the adoptive mother, greeting everybody cheerfully, walking in and out, smiling all the while. She acted, said the examining psychologist, for all the world like a prima donna or a famous actress, smiling at everybody, almost throwing kisses.

The child's behavior made sense. She had, of course, no way of knowing that her new parents were offering her a real home, and she was trying very hard, in self-defense, to keep her distance from them and from any adult. "Stay away from them the way they stay away from you." The adoptive parents were advised to tell Lois several times a day that she had come to stay with them forever. They were advised to speak to the child about her previous caregivers, in order to help her develop a sense that people continue to exist even when they are gone. They were advised to tell Lois that they loved her and that they would never, never, never leave her. The formula was repeated in many versions: you will be with us forever, this house is going to be here forever, this piano is going to stand here forever, this chair is going to be in this house forever, and so on. Within a month of this treatment by the adoptive parents, the child began to show her first spontaneous feelings. She became very anxious at each separation, and this escalated into a full, intense separation anxiety. She cried when the adoptive mother went out of the room, and mantra-like, she kept asking, "Where are you? Where are you? Where are you going? Where are you?," trying to assure herself that the mother had not abandoned her. The acute anxiety subsided after four months of patient, repeated assurance that her new parents loved her and would never leave her or let her go. And, finally, the child recovered her capacity to feel both love and pain.

What we are dealing with here seems like very simple treatment. It is simple. But a lot of treatment is simple, though it derives from a sophisticated understanding of the child and the meaning of her symptoms and the recognition by the clinician that a very young child can show a "false self" if she thinks it necessary to survive. It is important that the judge know that there is an adjustment period in a new home that takes time, and perhaps even be concerned and ask questions if the adjustment seems to occur overnight. The kind of help Lois received is not yet widely available, but it certainly could be cultivated, could be taught, could be available, and would be enormously helpful to these children. Placement in a secure home is often not enough, as it was not enough with little Lois, who could not believe, at 2 years, that anybody could love her for herself and want her to stay "forever." Custody with one parent or two parents is not enough after the child has witnessed repeated violence or very high conflict. Children need help in recovering their capacity to move forward, without fear that the past will recur. Few can heal themselves.

In the court that I've created in my mind, the judge would not know how to do the treatment, but he would know that it exists, and he would be in a position of leadership to ask the social agency about its availability and not just passively accept the agency's saying, "Oh, we don't have the budget" or, "We don't know anything about it." He would send them to find out about it and what it costs. A good parent would do no less.

And, finally, there is another compelling reason for moving quickly within the agency and the court to make permanent plans for the child. That is the child's sense of time. Adults tell time by carefully defined units, by calendar or clock. But that is not how we adults tell time when we're in love, or when our lover, husband, child is away from us, or when our son or daughter is away at war, or when we are waiting for the ambulance or the police car. Then time takes on a different dimension. Children live in the kind of time zone we live in when we are in love, or at war, or in an emergency. Children's sense of time, well into 7 and 8 years old, is governed by the internal press of their needs and their anxieties. When the parent is late, the child with a secure attachment is annoyed or anxious but not frantic, or she may be so absorbed in play that she does not notice. But the insecure child endures the sufferings of hell: "She won't come," he says. "He will disappoint me again," is the thought. "I will be abandoned." And because the child has no rational sense of time, and does not know that parents can be delayed for a thousand and one reasons that have nothing to do with not loving him, his suffering is so much greater.

Children who are insecurely attached, as most of our charges are, can only stand to be separated from the attachment figure for a little while before they become withdrawn, depressed, or numbed in their feelings, like little Lois. In the days when children were admitted to the hospital and parents were not allowed to visit because hospital authorities insisted they would bring in germs, children took forever to get well. They languished in their cribs, barely eating, listless, and seemingly in despair. Then when hospitals changed, and parents were allowed in to visit, children began to recover quickly. They were no longer hospital orphans; they were loved; they had someone to get well for.

In their classic books, Goldstein, Solnit, and Freud proposed statutes that would assure that if a 3-year-old or younger child spent a year living in a foster home, or for a 6-year-old double that time, the foster home should be regarded as superseding the child's absent parent. They proposed that the child's sense of time should guide the court to a compassionate policy that would not forfeit a child's attachment to his new caregivers in order to privilege the natural parent–child relationship. They proposed further that the critical factor for assessment should be the length of time that the child spends continuously with the new caregivers, not the time away from the natural parents. It is the task of the judge—to quote Judge Leonard Edwards again—"to keep his or her eye on how fast the case moves, or slowly winds its way through the courts." For infants and toddlers, we have learned that a few days absent from the attached figure will feel like an eternity. For a child below age 5, the absence of a parent for more than two months is beyond comprehension. For the young child there is hardly a distinction between a short interval and a long absence. In accord with this thinking, when placement plans are made, the judge should be responsible for asking the social agency what difficulties they anticipate, and what plans they have ready to deal with these problems should they arise. To take this further, if and when the placement collapses, the judge should expect to receive clarification of what happened, and whether indeed the assessment of the family or the child was at fault, and how this situation could be avoided in the future. In sum, the judge needs to keep the real flesh-and-blood child in mind, not the voluminous case record. And, in the absence of good parents, the child needs to have someone proactive on his behalf, who can keep the system moving at the needed pace for his best interests.

I remember a very troubled child I worked with many years ago. He was 8. When I told him I was going on vacation for two weeks, he asked me for an electric extension cord, which I brought to the following session. He "plugged" one socket into my arm, and the other into his, and he said, happily, that now we would not be separated for even a day. He was right. Moreover he was recovering. He had begun to trust that a human connection can survive separation.

I turn now, all too briefly, to the parents. Attachment, of course, is a mutual creation of primary caregiver and child. There are many interferences with the parent's capacity to attach to a child that are unrelated to drugs or alcohol. Attachment problems, in adults, long predate drug problems, and occur in countries where alcohol is not common. I address here the ghosts that rise up out of the past of the parent when the child is born. If the mother, or the father, has had a good, or even adequate experience as a baby and child, that memory is a benign ghost that haunts the nursery. Throughout the nine months of pregnancy, the mother thinks with some apprehensiveness, but mainly with excitement and wonder, about the expected arrival. When the baby kicks inside her, she thinks happily that it's a strong baby. And when the baby appears, she looks at him and says, "Isn't he beautiful?—just like I always wanted. He's going to be a great poet, a scientist, maybe even a great judge." If the baby is relatively easy to care for and nurses well, this confirms her view: "He loves me," she says happily to herself, "and I love him." And the mutual relationship, of central significance to the child's life, and to the mother's life, is launched. The path is easier to trace with the mother than with the father, because she has the advantage of nine months of preparation, when her body and her whole being changed to get ready for the child. But the father's attitude as well is strongly influenced by his own experiences as a small child.

But if the mother has had a wretched infancy and childhood, there is another kind of ghost in the nursery. "Nobody ever loved you," says the ghost, "even when you were a baby." And throughout the whole nine months, the mother worries, "Will he be normal? Will he have ten fingers and toes? Will he be flawed?" And most of all, "Will he love me, and will I be able to take care of him?" And if the child is difficult, has colic, is underweight, fails to nurse well, the new mother says to herself all too quickly, because she anticipated that this would happen, "He rejects me—just like everyone else. And I will reject him back." And the downward spiral begins here. I might mention also that the most difficult fathers to work with have been those who have themselves been deserted as young children. Their hurtful memories were still so green they could have happened yesterday. Several ran from parenthood after divorce or separation because of the remembered pain.

Fortunately, there are many possibilities and many interventions, because it is exactly here, where the troubled young mother and father greet the new baby, that there is the greatest chance to help parents and prevent harm to the child. And, of course, the unhappy parent, who expects ill, can have a lovely baby and feel at that moment that her luck has changed, and that she's finally on a good path. And the happy mother can have a premature or a sick child. We know a great deal about how to help new parents at this critical time. But sadly, we have very few programs in place, and what happens in the main is that the cycle of unhappiness continues.

It was discovered in a study at the Anna Freud Centre in London, several years ago, that if you interview pregnant young women about the history of their own early childhood, and, a year after the baby is born, examine the quality of the attachment between mother and child, the story told by the mother is remarkably similar to the attachment that has developed with her child. There is an intergenerational effect that keeps going, for good or for ill. The moral of these findings is that when we are truly able to help even one troubled child, we have the ability to break into an intergenerational cycle and interfere with the next round of grief that was waiting to happen. The Talmud was right when it told us, "If you save one person, you save the world."

JicaP Vol. 2, No. 2, 2002

Parent Work in Analysis: Children, Adolescents, and Adults. Part Three: Middle and Pretermination Phases

Jack Novick, Ph.D., and Kerry Kelly Novick

This paper continues our examination of parent work in the context of child, adolescent, and adult analysis (K. K. Novick and J. Novick 2002). Moving forward from focus on evaluation, recommendation, setting the frame, and beginning the treatment, here we look at the work of the middle and pretermination phases. As in our earlier discussions, an underlying assumption is that treatment goals include parent development and restoration of the parent–child relationship.

Dangers at the Entry into the Middle Phase—Psychological Separation

In the last paper we described the case of Mark, a suicidal adolescent who, after a difficult beginning phase, developed an interest in the workings of his own mind and began to enjoy hopes and plans, all markers of entry for the individual patient into the middle phase of treatment. As he began to reject parental externalizations and become his own person, his parents were unable to tolerate his growing psychological autonomy and literally kidnapped him from treatment. Mark's case highlights the danger of a unilateral, premature termination at the beginning of the middle phase. As many do, his parents thought they could prevent psychological separation by controlling physical proximity. Parents may push for premature termination when there is symptomatic improvement, and avoid making the transition to supporting the child's growing autonomy.

Child analysts, who tend to identify with the child, may get very angry with parents at this point, feeling that the parents are sabotaging the child's efforts to use the treatment to grow up. It is crucial for the analyst to be able to empathize with parents' fear and sadness in their belief that any separation, physical or psychological, means losing their child. Here the prior work during the evaluation and recommendation bears fruit in our being able to remind parents that our goal is not only to restore the child to the path of progressive development, but also to restore their relationship to closeness on a new level.

Damian, 10, was so sad and constricted at the beginning of treatment that he told the analyst that he thought his family would be better off without him. He was an only child, much loved by his high-achieving parents, whose standards were impossibly exalted for both themselves and Damian. A lot of prior work with the parents helped them to set more realistic goals and enjoy Damian's increasing relaxation. But, as he began tentatively to pursue his own intellectual interests instead of their ambitions, they started complaining about the burden of treatment. Now that Damian was not overtly miserable, they wanted to stop. The analyst agreed that Damian was indeed looking happier on the outside, and reminded the parents of their earlier shared treatment goal of fostering increasing freedom of Damian's thinking and creativity, as well as a flourishing relationship with his parents. The analyst wondered about the parents' plan to have Damian cut short his pursuit of his creative interests.

The transformations that had been worked on during the evaluation and beginning phases included Damian's parents realizing that many of their feelings had an impact on him. The mother then spontaneously wondered what it might be in her that was creating such pressure to bring the treatment to a premature close. The therapist asked if she were again afraid she was going to lose her child. This intervention was based on the therapist's association to material in the developmental history about the mother's miscarriage before Damian's birth. Her response, however, was a surprise. She cried and said, "Like I lost the other two." She then explained that she had had an abortion when Damian was under a year old, because she thought and had been told that it would be too difficult to manage two infants. "It was the worst mistake of my life." In subsequent work, it became clear that Damian stood as a double replacement child for her. The parent work became emotionally intense over the next few months as they used the sessions to talk about and mourn the losses, but there was no longer any mention of ending Damian's treatment.

The transition from the beginning to middle phases is a peak of resistance, with the danger that parents will unilaterally end the treatment. Once parents' fear of loss can be addressed, children and adolescents usually settle into the long middle phase of work exploring the intrapsychic world. In many therapies this has been the time when parent work, if done at all, is set aside, or diminishes to meetings a few times in the year for informational catching-up. Therapists may prefer to turn their attention to the unfolding of the child's inner life and experience parents as irrelevant or a hindrance.

Our view is otherwise: we suggest that the middle phase brings with it a series of important tasks in the alliance with parents which, if engaged with, can consolidate the adult in the phase of parenthood, allow for dealing with subtle parental resistances that can stalemate the child's treatment, and help ensure that the therapy will proceed to a useful termination with continued positive growth beyond the end of treatment.

By the middle of a treatment, parents who have worked consistently with the child or adolescent's therapist through the earlier phases have addressed their extreme feelings of failure and transformed their guilt into usable concern. They have begun to regain a sense of competence as parents, and can begin to see their children as separate from themselves, which allows for starting to master the tasks of psychological separation from the child and allowing the patient to be with another adult and to begin to form a significant relationship.

Allowing for psychological separation, individuation, and autonomy is the primary task for parents during the middle phase, accomplished by working collaboratively with the therapist. But this also brings with it specific anxieties, conflicts, and defenses in the parents, which can give rise to resistances, stalemates, and premature termination. We can characterize three problematic parent dynamics that will have to be addressed in the middle phase. One is parental decathexis or disinvestment of the child, followed by displacement. The second is parents' protection of their own personality structures, particularly characteristic defenses and superego configurations. Children are often drawn into or collude with this defensive protection. Third is parental resistance to the revival and potential revision of issues from their own histories.

The middle phase of any treatment brings with it a deepening of material and increased complexity of dynamics. This is certainly true in child and adolescent therapies; the addition of parental conflicts and resistances, and their interaction with the child in treatment, makes the therapist's work ever more challenging. As we noted in the earlier papers in this series (J. Novick and K. K. Novick 2001, K. K. Novick and J. Novick 2002), we have found the interlocking conceptual frameworks of two systems of self-regulation and the therapeutic alliance tasks of different phases of treatment very helpful. But it is important to note that these are only models, devised to operate as internal mental maps or signposts for the analyst through the journey of the analysis. They provide for us an articulation of the goals of treatment and generate technical interventions that address multiple dimensions of clinical phenomena. Accomplishment of therapeutic alliance tasks by child, parents, or therapist both springs from and conduces to open-system functioning, which in turn allows for ongoing measurement of therapeutic progress.

Therapeutic Alliance Tasks of the Middle Phase

Parent Tasks

As noted above, the task of parents during the middle phase of their child's treatment is to allow for exploration and the growth of autonomy, individuality, and psychological separation. We look for parents' increasing ability to facilitate and enjoy the child or adolescent's separateness by supporting the child's new ways of being, the child's new adaptations, including more adaptive ways of coping with internal and external stresses. Parents are learning to balance the sadness of their feelings of loss with pleasure in the child's growth. They become open to pleasant surprise at the child's new interests and blossoming talents, joining the child in new modes of relating.

This growth on the part of parents involves their becoming aware of possible choices between what we have termed "open" and "closed" systems of regulation of relations with the self and with others. As we noted in Parent Work II (K. K. Novick and J. Novick 2002),

> Woven throughout our work with patients of different ages and pathologies, and now applied to work with parents, is a set of hypotheses concerning self-regulation and sources of self-esteem in everyone. Faced with experiences of helplessness, from whatever source, every person has to find a way to cope and feel good. These adaptations can be constructive and creative, building what we have called an "open system" of self-regulation. Alternatively and simultaneously, at any point in development, the individual has available pathological solutions based on omnipotent defenses, which we have described as a "closed system."

The quality and form of love in relationships, including those between parents and between parents and child, relates to these two systems. Mutually enhancing relationships stem from and produce open-system functioning and growth, while closed-system functioning conduces to and is reinforced by sadomasochistic patterns of relating (Novick and Novick 1991, 1994, 1996a,b, 2000). Thus we might characterize the goals of treatment for parents in terms of their movement out of closed-system functioning with their child to more open-system self-regulation and relationship with each other and with the child (J. Novick and K. K. Novick 2002). For example, parents can choose between old power struggles with their child and novel, mutually respectful and loving negotiations within realistic boundaries set by reality and parental authority.

THERAPIST TASKS

The therapist's goal in the middle phase is to help parents move toward the possibility of more open-system functioning. We have many techniques available for this work. There are *educative* interventions, such as explaining the difference between an authoritarian stance, in which a parent arbitrarily exercises the power of his age and strength, and an authoritative one, in which he uses his knowledge to explain and teach the child about the situation. *Support* and *validation* are central needs of parents that therapists meet by empathic *verbalization* of feelings, and *tracking* of emerging open-system functioning, as when a parent shows pleasure in the child. *Modeling* different ways to think about the child's behavior and feelings, and to talk with the child provides parents with powerful examples of effective relating. *Facilitating* parents' finding more adaptive ways to respond to and interact with the child involves fostering realistic mutual identifications in place of relationships based on externalizations.

Parent Work as Therapy

Child and adolescent therapists have always used these techniques with parents, but have suffered from lack of a conceptual framework and therefore no sense of permission to be explicit about it. Even more vexing and little-discussed is the substantive therapeutic dimension of parent work. Despite the ubiquity of therapeutic interventions with parents in practice (see, for example, Anna Freud's work with Peter Heller's father in conjunction with her analysis of the then 8-year-old Peter, described in Heller 1990), child analysts and therapists have no coherent theoretical model to encompass this work. We suggest that the concept of the therapeutic alliance tasks and the treatment goals of parental restoration to the path of progressive adult development within the context of their child's or adolescent's treatment provide the beginning of such a model.

This brings us then to the application of the whole repertoire of clinical techniques in parent work. We can illustrate their relevance and utility both by the difficulties that arise when the therapist pulls back from using these skills and, in the positive sense, when *interpretation* and *working through* are crucial to the success of both of the dual goals of treatment. In our experience, use of the full range of therapeutic techniques in parent work does not compete or interfere with individual therapy for parents. Indeed, parent work may lead to acceptance of a referral for individual treatment while maintaining the relationship with the child analyst for work on parenting issues. Parent work focuses on the parent–child relationship; other issues in the parents' lives are engaged with only as they have relevance to their relationship with their child. Thus we may use the full range of our skills without inhibition in the very limited and focused area of parenting. In past work (Novick and Novick 1996b), we have emphasized the importance of child experience for adult work, but parent work of the middle phase of a child or adolescent treatment calls especially upon the adult experience of the therapist.

Parenting difficulties were the focus in a therapist's work with the mother of Lucy, a very disturbed 9-year-old. The mother started each parent session by externalizing her good parenting functions onto the analyst, presenting her failures in a self-denigrating way. Over time the analyst interpreted the mother's guilt at not protecting her daughter from the father's abusive style, and the self-punishment in the mother's externalizations. This work enabled the mother to acknowledge and use her own capacities with her child, making psychological space for the child's treatment to proceed well. The persistence of the problems with her husband, however, led the mother to seek her own treatment, with the child analyst's support and approval. At this point, however, the child's therapist backed off, feeling concerned that continued therapeutic work might interfere with the mother's own treatment. The child analyst stopped seeing Lucy's mother, who clearly expressed her hurt and anger. Rather than continuing work on restoring the parenting function, the therapist relied on the mother's own treatment to do the whole job. Soon afterward, in a joint session with the parents, the father summarily ended the treatment, while the mother sat by apparently helplessly. It became clear that the mother had engineered the sudden premature termination—she had dropped the therapist as she had felt dropped and the opportunity to treat both child and parents was lost.

Parental Withdrawal from the Child

There are often important dynamic issues underlying the tendency to a relative shift to exclusive focus on the child's inner world during the middle phase of treatment at the expense of continuing parent work. The child's or adolescent's increasing psychological separateness confronts parents with their own personality limitations, often reviving painful issues from their own pasts. The child's growth can represent a massive assault on the adult's characteristic defenses, superego configurations, and modes of dealing with painful or traumatic experiences. If the therapist engages the parents during this phase of the child's therapy there is a risk of a major counterattack. Conscious or unconscious worry about this may contribute to the therapist's avoidance of continuing work. Parental self-protection may not necessarily take a blatant behavioral form, however, but may appear as a withdrawal of investment in the child.

> Eight-year-old John, the child of divorced parents, was sometimes brought to his session by his father. There was a lot of giggling, wrestling, and physical contact whenever they were together in the waiting room. During the first year of treatment, the therapist had worked with John around new ways of making friends and doing better at school. The therapist noticed that every time father brought John, he entered the session regressed, provocative, and unable to work. When his mother brought him he functioned at his most advanced level. In John's session, the therapist remarked on this contrast and wondered aloud if all the physical activity with his dad was upsetting to John. John denied this in the session, but asked his father to stop wrestling. In the next regular parent session, John's father told the therapist that he thought his son didn't love him any more, but that he didn't mind so much since he had his younger son and could now love him.
>
> In this situation the therapist could clearly track the sequence from the pathological mode of relating, John's effort to separate himself from his father's use of him, the withdrawal of investment in John by the father, and the subsequent reexternalization of excitement onto his next child. First the

analyst questioned the father's assertion that John did not love him. Father's belief that love is equivalent to sadomasochistic enmeshment could be made explicit. Father then volunteered the memory that this was the way he related with his own father and older brothers.

The father and the therapist then began to explore other ways of loving, more in tune with John's own interests. Father took John to a car dealer with him when he was shopping for a new car and they shared their likes and dislikes. The relationship began to change to a warmer, more age-appropriate interaction. Soon after this, the father asked for a referral to begin his own therapy while continuing in parent work.

Sometimes, however, parental withdrawal is more subtle. The parents do not oppose the treatment and seem cooperative. The initial worries of the beginning phase seem over, the child is improving, and the analyst may feel that there seems to be little need to meet, indeed, may have a sense that there is not quite enough to talk about. We have come to think that this feeling may indicate a danger point. Experience of extreme reactions to progress, such as in the case of Mark, the adolescent described in the last paper (K. K. Novick and J. Novick 2002), whose parents kidnapped him when he began to change, has alerted us to pay particular attention to parental reactions to the child or adolescent's initial moves toward autonomy. We quickly note and question reactions.

In a meeting a week after the analyst had described to her parents how well 8-year-old Amy was beginning to work things out on her own in treatment, the mother looked depressed. The analyst noted her mood and invited her to talk about it. At first Amy's mother denied feeling "down." Then she said she had been "feeling a little logy" and wondered if she might be getting the flu. When the therapist then said that actually she sounded sad, the mother's eyes began to tear. "You're right," she said. "I hadn't noticed it but I do feel sad, and I don't know why." After they explored together some other possible sources, the analyst remarked that they had talked the previous week about an important growing-up step taken by their daughter; the analyst noted that it is quite usual for parents to react to their child's forward moves with pride and pleasure, but also with sadness.

The parent session ended with the mother feeling much lighter, but, the next week, she said that she was continuing to struggle with periods of sadness. "I feel as if I've lost something, I don't know what." The analyst suggested that they think together about autonomy and what it meant to the parents. Amy's mother and father talked about their own experiences in adolescence, when their parents had reacted with rejection and hostility to their growing independence, treating them as if they were abandoning the family. As they described the guilt and anger connected with these issues, the analyst helped them realize that they had internalized their parents' reactions and were repeating their own attachment histories with Amy (Fonagy et al. 1993).

This difficult and powerful therapeutic work began to address an intense conflict for both of Amy's parents. On the one hand they felt the need to maintain a sense of connection with their own parents, bolstered by externalizations, and to defend against guilt at potentially surpassing their parents, avoided by pathological generalizations. On the other hand, they deeply wanted to create a space for their little girl to blossom, and to feel good as parents. Without direct work on these issues, parents desperately protecting their own characteristic defenses might have prematurely terminated Amy's treatment.

STALEMATE

Even when a treatment continues, there is a serious danger of stalemate in the child's therapy if the therapist avoids addressing central parental conflicts. Amy's parents, in their fear and anger that her independent growth constituted a hostile rejection of them, consciously or unconsciously created Amy's (and every child's) worst nightmare—that they would emotionally withdraw from and abandon her. Children who pick up this danger usually react with their own version of withdrawal, retreating from the therapist and the therapy, which both represent progressive development. This can also take the form of apparent compliance, as we saw in the case of Damian, the very sad 10-year-old.

We noted earlier the intensification of the parent work when Damian's mother revealed her secret history of loss. Equally significant was the shift within Damian's therapy. Despite his increasing comfort and security in the sessions, there had still been a quality of rapid compliance with the parents that made it hard to discern the distinction between his psychic space and theirs. It was only after they could begin to see that they had externalized aspects of their own history, that Damian was carrying more sadness than a 10-year-old should, that he began to talk in his own sessions of ways in which he differed from his parents and how angry he felt when they assumed that they knew his wishes.

Protection of the Superego

In earlier papers (K. K. Novick and J. Novick 2002) we described interactions between five-year-old Henry's difficulties and his parents' problems, involving both externalizations and pathological identifications. Another issue arose in the middle phase.

> Henry's own therapy was proceeding, with work focused on his anxiety about bodily integrity, when his father complained bitterly in a parent session about Henry's "lying." Father felt that Henry, by then nearly 7 years old, constantly evaded the truth to avoid responsibility for his chores and homework, that Henry blamed others when he lost his backpack or jacket, and that Henry kept "fudging" the difference between real and pretend. The analyst agreed that these were serious issues and talked to the parents about Henry's struggles over his developing conscience, and how his thinking was sometimes drawn into his intense conflicts. In this context the analyst noted in a general way how important it was that his parents be clear and consistent about rules and realities.
>
> Henry's mother said she had been trying, but felt unsupported by her husband in this dimension. He indignantly protested when she detailed his flouting of rules and laws in front of the children, deciding arbitrarily when they should wear their seat belts, riding his bike without a helmet, changing their bedtime unexpectedly, and so forth. The analyst reminded the father of how closely Henry and he were identified with each other, and suggested that perhaps they also shared a problem about their consciences. Henry's father became quite angry and stopped coming to sessions for two months.
>
> At the next meeting the analyst apologized to Henry's mother for apparently touching a nerve with her husband. The mother did not want to talk at any length about it, although she seemed embarrassed by his absence and made an excuse for him. Rather, she was preoccupied with a surge in Henry's anxiety level and his reluctance to go to school. The analyst took her lead and focused for the next several sessions on understanding together how Henry's deep worries interfered with his capacity to use his ego to differentiate real and fantasied dangers. Then they moved to considering how the mother could help Henry enjoy the security of a predictable routine and expectations. As Henry relaxed within the safety of a more consistent daily experience, and both his mother and his father could see the difference, Henry's mother felt stronger in being able to advocate with her husband for an effort to set a better example. Henry's father returned to parent sessions and rejoined the work directly, more able to think at least about his son's developing superego.

This experience in the work with Henry and his parents shows how easily a challenge to a parent's superego configuration can potentially derail a treatment. In retrospect, it seems that the analyst moved too quickly into drawing the parallels between Henry's and his father's conflicts. The father reacted with angry defensive withdrawal and Henry's anxiety surged; without the mother's deep and somewhat desperate commitment, they might have stopped treatment at that point. What the analyst then did with Henry's mother, that is (1) to work explicitly to develop alternative solutions to Henry's superego conflicts; (2) to illuminate the cost to him of anxious, hostile, and punitive functioning and the gains of freer experimentation within a framework of safety; and (3) to move gradually to a perception of his parents' central importance as models and containers for him—all this might have been done with both parents. Focusing the parent work on the child with the understanding that one is also working in displacement on the parents' difficulties calls for the same kind of patience and timing that we use in individual work.

Severe Parental Pathology

Sometimes, however, the pathology or character issues of one parent may be such that it is impossible to work directly at all with both parents together. Rather than a temporary hiatus, as with Henry's parents, the analyst may have to work with and through only one parent for the whole time of treatment, as was the case with 4-year-old Davey.

> Davey's idealized father had left the family when Davey was 2. Despite the severity of Davey's aggressive and anxious symptoms, his father was vehemently opposed to treatment from the start. He refused to participate in any parent sessions, with or without his ex-wife. Davey's mother persisted, however, and made the decision to proceed with treatment. In the middle phase, when Davey greatly enjoyed his treatment and was changing visibly, including developing a clearer sense of himself, which in turn meant he saw his parents more realistically and had better inner controls, his father demanded that the analysis stop right away. Father also began to criticize the analyst to the child and tell Davey that he shouldn't go there any more. The analyst's efforts to have father come in to discuss the issues were fruitless.
>
> From what the analyst could discern, the interaction between Davey's parents was similar to the sadomasochistic battles Davey engaged in with his mother, in which she played the passive, helpless victim while covertly

enraging Davey. Mother constantly badgered her ex-husband to pay for Davey's treatment, although he had always refused and didn't actually have the resources. Rather than allowing himself to be rendered helpless and furious in this situation, the analyst suggested to the mother that she explain to Davey's father that the treatment would end much sooner if he supported it emotionally. She would not ask for financial support if he offered positive validation for Davey's own experience, but she would legally petition him for back child support and his financial responsibility for his child's treatment if he prolonged the treatment unnecessarily by putting the child in such an impossible loyalty conflict. Davey's father backed down and began to remark appropriately to Davey when he noticed him controlling his anger and excitement, attributing the changes to the hard work Davey was doing with his analyst.

This was a situation in which the sadomasochistic character pathology of both parents was so severe that it had to be addressed by confrontation. They had played interchangeable roles of bully and victim during their marriage and these roles persisted in their parenting afterwards. The work with Davey's mother throughout the treatment had, however, expanded her repertoire of realistic responses and healthy investment in her child. This allowed the analyst to work with her to support her addressing her ex-husband's destructiveness directly.

Sacrifice of the Child

The outcome is not always so positive when middle phase work threatens long-standing role relationships in a marriage or family. A family secret that can no longer be denied, or abuse in the past or present, can become the focus of intense parental efforts to maintain the status quo and resist the impact for change that comes from a child's treatment. We have written about the negative therapeutic motivation (Novick and Novick 1996b), with which a parent brings a child to treatment in order to make the analyst fail, and to preserve a pathological, usually externalizing, relationship. We can now extend this idea to include the parents' effort to use the child in a new way to protect a pathological family structure. In open-system development parents and children change with each other as each develops into new phases. A perversion of that process occurs when a family that has found a pathological equilibrium that is then disrupted by developmental changes or external imperatives, like school entrance, reconstitutes around new sado-masochistic patterns, as we saw in the case of Kenny.

Six-year-old Kenny had suffered from his mother's screaming rages and his father's wildly sadistic teasing and overwhelming through most of his life. When he entered treatment he was unable to stay alone in a room, toilet himself, go to school, or sleep in his own bed. He also could not be left alone with his little brother without attacking him mercilessly. After a year of analysis, with weekly parent sessions, Kenny had greatly improved. He was attending school, had mastered toileting, could play at another child's house, and woke only a few times in the night. This excellent progress had been achieved through analysis of his murderous terror and its underlying omnipotent belief in the power of his aggression, and through painstaking parent guidance around basic issues of routine and respectful interchange.

What had not changed much was Kenny's mistreatment of his brother and his parents' embarrassment in front of their friends and family at Kenny's relatively high anxiety level about anything and everything. The parents' emphasis on how humiliated and ashamed they felt elicited the analyst's empathy, as well as a sense that such intense shame intimated the fear of having something exposed. In exploring this, both the mother's and father's rage at Kenny for making them "look so bad" emerged with renewed force. It was as if the ordinary guilt they had felt, which had been worked with throughout, was just the top layer. Underneath was a certainty that they really were going to be shown to be terrible parents. This fear masked an omnipotent conviction that they had a right to use Kenny as they wished. They had spoken of many incidents of humiliating Kenny with teasing—father always shook his head ruefully, telling the analyst he knew he would get in trouble in the session for these things. Mother had cried over her knowledge that screaming at him only made Kenny more scared.

The analyst had worked with the parents around their household organization, in which the mother felt unsupported, as she carried full domestic responsibility while the father worked very long hours and pursued a time-consuming hobby outside the home. Matters came to a head when the father went on one of his frequent business trips, leaving the mother alone with two difficult small children and no household help, although the family could well afford it. Kenny's anxiety peaked whenever his father was not there to protect him in the night. Kenny acted out in school and the teacher called his mother in at the end of the day, in front of other parents. She was humiliated and enraged, feeling that she and her child were singled out, and, at the same time, that Kenny deserved severe punishment rather than the understanding that was counseled by the analyst. When the father returned, he confined Kenny to his room, which produced angry, hysterical panic and tantrums. The exhausted child finally went to sleep, but his father woke him for school by pouring cold water over him in bed, which produced another panicky outburst.

Despite feeling very angry, indignant, and worried about Kenny, the analyst was able to see that the mother felt helplessly overwhelmed, and that the father was in the grip of a compulsion he could not control. The analyst tried to elucidate for them the impact of their handling on Kenny and what was understood from his sessions, but both parents were adamant in their stance that Kenny was the villain of the piece. Another tack taken in the parent work was to support the mother in her articulation of her practical and emotional needs, in parallel with Kenny's work on saying in words what he felt and wanted.

At this juncture Kenny's analysis had proceeded to the point where old structures within him were shifting, but this meant he was rejecting blanket externalizations from each parent, was protesting when his autonomy was attacked, and was seeking alternative sources of gratification outside the sadomasochistic interaction within the family. His parents could not tolerate the changes this demanded from them. Kenny was too important as a target for externalizations to their individual personality structures and to the secret abusive power gratifications within their marriage. Rather than risk exposure and the attendant demand to change, they sacrificed Kenny and the treatment, removing him summarily.

Guilt and Remorse

A major issue in parent work during the middle phase touches on the distinction between guilt and remorse. Remorse is a feeling that accompanies open-system functioning, in that it recognizes the reality of our helplessness to undo the past. Guilt, on the other hand, includes an omnipotent assumption of responsibility and denial of the reality of time. With a setting aside of the omnipotent quality of the feeling of guilt, a person is left with remorse. With remorse, reparation becomes possible. In a family context of the reality of sins of omission or commission in the past, reparation can be considered in terms of what can actually be done currently.

Despite the limitations of reality, parents can be helped to take a series of reparative steps. First there has to be an acknowledgment to the child of past wrongdoing. For instance, we can help a parent to recognize that even being a passive bystander while someone else was abusive allowed the abuse to occur. As we saw in the partially failed case of Kenny, this is often done to protect oneself or the marriage. This emerged clearly also in work with the adolescent Mark.

> It was an important and dramatic period in the parent work when Mark's father faced the fact that he had stood passively by. He had sacrificed his son for his own safety and self-defense. His wife accused Mark and treated him like a monster in the service of her rage against men. After several meetings' therapeutic work on her relationship with her son, Mark's mother turned her rage on the father, threatened divorce, insisted that they sleep in separate bedrooms, and stopped coming to parent sessions.
>
> Soon after this, the father called Mark's analyst in some distress. He said that he could not sleep for thinking about what he had allowed his wife to do to Mark. What could he do? At this point Mark's analysis had slowed down, with Mark missing sessions or zoning out during them, especially at moments of work on his anger with his parents. Mark only occasionally had access to his rage at his father—he said his father was still being passive. Father and son were uncomfortable talking with each other, usually provoking disputes. Each would leave conversations feeling angry and disappointed.
>
> The analyst responded to the father's plea by suggesting a joint session with father, Mark, and therapist. The meeting started with Mark looking sullen and father unable to meet his eye. Father then began to talk about his realization that he had not only left Mark unprotected, but had done it for selfish reasons, because he was afraid of mother's rage. Mark seemed startled at first, but then retreated behind a wall of words, complaining that it was "too little, too late." Father mumbled, "I know," and slumped further down in his chair.
>
> The therapist noted that father's acknowledgment had taken some courage and was an important first step. Father straightened up and began to talk. He noted his inability to undo the past and apologized with deep sorrow and regret for what his son had endured because of him. He looked at Mark and said, "I have always loved you, but I think my actions, or rather inactions, made a huge wall between us. Can we try to become friends now?"
>
> Mark sat silently for a while, then said, "I think I have always hoped you would say this, but, more, I also hoped you would rescue me, go back and make it never have happened. I guess I have to give up that magic wish."

Tears came to the eyes of both as Mark said, "This is good." Both men were "tough guys" who had always zoned out rather than show any feelings. To the surprise of all three in the room, they reached out for a handshake, then rose to hug each other, and both cried for the rest of the session. Mark and his father no longer needed the therapist's active presence in joint sessions to continue to work on developing their relationship.

A further reparative step that the analyst can encourage is parental awareness of the continuing impact in the present of past events, and sensitivity to related current difficulties. Then parents can do something ameliorative in the present. After the work described above, Mark and his father could react together to current conflicts and Mark's self-destructive behavior in a different way.

Another effect of this work was to break the deadlock in Mark's own treatment. He began to reflect on his continuing need to see himself as the victim of an abusive mother. Mark wondered if this kept alive his magical thoughts about being rescued. He said, "I could probably keep this up forever, but what's it getting me? It's an endless cycle of suffering, getting overwhelmed with rage, zoning out and then having to work so hard to come alive again. It's a waste, I have too much I love to do."

Pretermination

Mark's treatment moved quickly, with visible effects outside. He carved out a very lucrative, unique, and creative career that used his full intellectual capacities. He started a new relationship on the basis of thinking about the long term, rather than just the need to prove himself attractive. He seemed to understand and relate to his mother in a different way, one that encompassed the complexity of his personality, their interaction, and their history. He had earlier dropped out of college, part of his inability to finish anything, but he arranged to complete his studies. Both Mark and the analyst began to think about his finishing treatment.

Mark was thinking of stopping and the analyst was thinking about assessing together Mark's readiness to begin a termination phase. This is the work of pretermination, testing capacities to address the exciting and difficult work of termination. The pretermination phase is seldom written about in the psychoanalytic literature. When it is, it is rarely conceptualized as having its own specific features, tasks, anxieties, or conflicts. We have described the importance of defining a pretermination phase of treatment in which both patient and analyst can explore whether they are ready to enter into and make maximum use of the termination period (Novick and Novick 1996b, 1998).

Criteria for starting a termination phase differ significantly from the criteria used at the end of treatment to assess the relative success of the work (Novick 1982, 1990, Novick and Novick 2001). Making the judgment tends to be intuitive, with criteria based on a sense of movement or momentum, that is, a sense that progressive development is reinstated. We note an increase in pleasure, joy, creativity, and autonomous, independent use of capacities, all hallmarks of open-system functioning. Either the patient, the analyst, or both begin to think that an ending might be possible.

Without setting a date, the analyst and patient discuss what will be involved, with the analyst describing in general terms how this part of the work can be structured and what can be accomplished. The analyst emphasizes the termination period as one of hard work that can bring great benefits. It is a time of consolidating therapeutic gains and internalizing the accomplishment of the therapeutic alliance tasks in the context of saying goodbye. This description prompts a joint assessment of work accomplished, work remaining, and a catalogue of capacities that will be called upon to do the work of termination.

Just the mention of termination often brings powerful reactions. The roots of these contain the potential for premature termination, forced by either patient or analyst, in the service of defensive avoidance on either side of renewed separation issues. The risk of ruining a good treatment is very high at this point.

PARENT WORK DURING PRETERMINATION

But what about parents? In the usual structure of parent work parents are often seen infrequently during the middle phase and then demand ending of treatment just at the point when pretermination ought to be initiated by patient and analyst. In such situations parents are anticipating an ending and seizing control of the process. Here it is useful to call upon the concept of a pretermination phase and to explain its importance to parents, so that they can again be enlisted to work together toward a planned termination phase.

Regular work with parents throughout the treatment usually prevents a preemptive strike and a premature termination. Indeed, we have often experienced a different response. Some parents, when told that ending is on the horizon, say, "Don't rush it" or "Don't rock the boat when everything is going so smoothly."

> Mark's parents were relieved and pleased with their new level of relationship with him. Mother was seldom so angry at him, and father and son were sharing many interests and frequently supported each other in their separate endeavors. When it was discussed in a parent session that it seemed that Mark was moving into a pretermination phase, his mother expressed concern about rushing things. His father said to the analyst, "I know you've been seeing him for a long time, and you must be getting bored or impatient, but do you think it's wise to end before we're sure there won't be a relapse?"

The first task for the analyst was to help them with their anxiety that, without treatment and the analyst, Mark would revert to his suicidal, sadomasochistic functioning. They lacked confidence that he and they could independently sustain a loving relationship.

At this point Mark was 21, chronologically an adult, but his parents still paid a large proportion of the cost of his treatment. Most child analysts, trained as we were too, tend to stay at arm's length from the parents of their adolescent patients. Work with Mark and other young adults has led us to reconsider this position and we now routinely find ways to work with the parents of adolescents.

> During the early years of Mark's analysis, Mark had participated in the weekly parent sessions, but he soon realized that the focus was on their parenting skills. As the parent work had deepened and turned to the parents' own conflicts about being good parents, Mark felt that his presence was inhibiting their work. He knew that his individual work was private, but that the analyst would share with him aspects of the parent work if it seemed it would be helpful to his growth. Further, Mark and his parents knew that joint meetings were possible whenever they wanted.
>
> In the middle phase of Mark's treatment, his parents kept contact with the analyst and conducted their work by phone, email, and monthly meetings. Periodically, Mark asked about the goals of the parent work, as he realized that his parents' specific goals changed as he changed. Mark helped to articulate his parents' tasks for each phase of his treatment.
>
> As Mark's pretermination work intensified he suggested to the analyst that he thought his parents needed to be seen more often again, as he

thought they felt unready to have him finish his treatment. He was picking up their difficulty in the pretermination parent task of, in Furman's (1992) words, "standing by to admire." This task demands of the parents (and of the analyst) that they forgo the intense gratification of doing for and doing with the child, in favor of meeting the child's need to have the parents and other important people take pleasure in his feelings of mastery and achievements, to appreciate his creativity and accomplishments, to trust him and encourage him in moments of frustration, and to allow him to develop confidence in himself.

Mark's parents struggled with their old propensity to fear Mark's skills and competence as destructive and hostile, thus confirming his omnipotent belief in his destructiveness. In standing by to admire they were recognizing and respecting his separate positive capacities. But they were also allowing him to experience his pathological omnipotent sadomasochistic beliefs as his own construction, which he alone could choose to set aside or retain.

The analyst first took up Mark's parents' anxiety by affirming that nothing would be decided until they could explore the reasons for their concern. Their most conscious worry was that the end would come upon them quickly, without careful consideration. Although these perceptions informed the analyst's thinking, the analyst did not enter into what by then was their familiar obsessionality, their inability to make decisions about anything, their counterreactive impulsivity, followed by years of regret. Rather, the analyst stayed on the level of providing a general explanation of how long treatments end and the importance of the termination period for consolidating the positive gains. The pretermination period was described as the time for assessing readiness for a termination period and doing what would be needed to make the termination beneficial to everyone. This provided immediate reassurance, which allowed the analyst to then shift the focus to the parents' tasks during this phase, with the idea that they could work to consolidate the gains they had made in their parenting. An immediate difficulty arose, as Mark's mother continued to resist any work that might threaten her defensive position of blamelessness for any of Mark's past difficulties. She continued to feel that he had been a monster; she thought that the positive change in their relationship was a result of his "at last coming to his senses" and deciding at least to act in a civilized manner. She appreciated the work Mark had done in therapy, but found little value in the parent work. She was relieved that there would not be a precipitate ending and hoped that there would be no reversion to his "throwing fits" as soon as treatment ended.

Parents and analyst decided that the father would continue to attend parent sessions regularly and convey important things to the mother. The door was left open for her attendance at any time. In the next session alone, Mark's father talked about his sense that his wife could not manage any threat to her externalizing, blaming style. He noted that he protects Mark and accepts that, at times, he has to "serve as the bad guy. That's the way she is and she won't change. There always has to be some bad man out there to blame." Work focused on the realignment in the family, with the father taking on an active role in realistic rescue and protection of the children from the abusive mother.

Father emailed his insight that one of his worries about the end of Mark's treatment was that he would "be out of a job. If Mark doesn't need to stay in treatment, if he can take care of himself, then he doesn't need me to protect him and then what's left? Wow! I have to keep him a helpless child so that I can be a valued father. What a crock of shit! Mark and I have so much more going for us. I realized that my anxiety about his mother was really an anxiety about the end of my usefulness. What else is there? See you next week."

Before the next meeting, the father wrote, "There is more—my envy. How I wish that I could have had analysis at his age. Perhaps I could have been as happy and creative and productive as he is. Isn't it strange to envy my own son even when he is benefiting from what I have provided for him? What next? See you Tuesday."

Next was the father's awareness of how angry he felt with his own father, who had been the passive bystander while his wife (Mark's grandmother) controlled and abased the children. He was angry and sad during the session. He said, "I don't know how many generations of my family men carried on the pattern of marrying powerful, controlling, abusive women and stood by as their own children were destroyed. I've been in my own therapy for years. I've been helped in many ways. I'm very grateful, but it's only in our work together on my parenting that I could see and feel this repeated pattern of allowing our sons to be abused. I hope that it's not too late to stop this. I hope the change in my relationship with Mark can provide him with a different model of how a father can be." He then wondered if he could get enough done before Mark finished treatment.

The therapist said that they would work until the end, but, if necessary, they could continue working on parent issues after Mark terminated. Father seemed pleased that he wasn't working under a time constraint, but then canceled the next session, claiming pressing business needs. That evening he emailed, "I'm sure you didn't believe the bullshit about work. I did have urgent matters, but I always do. I had convinced myself that I couldn't spare the time. I first realized that I couldn't bear the thought of Mark surpassing me—being more successful, happier, and nicer than I am. But then it struck me that I'm talking about my surpassing my father. This is an issue I've worked on in my own therapy, but never in terms of my being a better father. For years I've worked on my guilt for surpassing my father physically, sexually, academically, financially. This must be the last battle. A part of me wants to be as bad a father as my dad was with me. Can we meet an extra time this next week?"

At the next few meetings, Mark's father spoke of his enjoyment spending time with his son. "It's like having a fascinating friend. I love to listen to him talk about his work and his life. I don't mind when I have little to add. It's just wonderful to listen to him. I feel so proud of him. His new venture is filled with risks but I'm confident he'll make it work."

Soon after, Mark cleared the last hurdle of the pretermination phase. He felt ready and confident to start a time of saying goodbye. In the next week he chose a date three months ahead for finishing his analysis and the termination period could begin.

This intensive period of work with Mark and his parents was crucial to the completion of his treatment and the restoration to progressive development of both the adolescent and his parents. Despite the handicap of their individual histories, Mark's parents entered into the work to each of their fullest capacity. His mother was unable to bear working directly, but she tolerated and appreciated the changes in the other family members over time. To the extent she was able, she made use indirectly of the insights achieved in the parent work. Mark's father made crucial leaps forward in his own therapy under the impetus of the parent work, and was able to bring these gains into his personal life and his parenting, to Mark's great benefit.

From the analyst's point of view, the technical issues in the pretermination phase with Mark's parents involved letting each of them, particularly the father, work as independently as they could, while providing support and "standing by to admire" them as well. What is important to underline here, however, is how active this stance is, how work with parents continues to be important and intense even in the closing stages of treatment, and even in work with adolescents and young adults.

Applications to Adult Treatment

Conceptualizing the pretermination phase as a unique period in treatment, with specific tasks and conflicts, is valuable in general in work with adults as well as in work with children and parents (Novick 1997, Novick and Novick 1996b, 2001). From this current discussion on parent work during the pretermination phase we can draw two particular significant applications to individual work with adults. The first is the danger of premature termination at the transition from the middle to pretermination. The second concerns various resistances to picking a date and starting the termination phase.

In the paper on evaluation we described how adult patients may use their significant others as objects for externalization of important functions of the internalized parent representations. It is useful to keep this in mind throughout the treatment, and to monitor how adult patients are able appropriately to include important people in their lives in the progress of their treatment and development. We noted in this paper that parents who have not been adequately included in work throughout treatment may feel threatened by their child or adolescent's independence and psychological separateness. They may react by ending treatment abruptly and so trying to return their child to the orbit of a closed system of sadomasochistic control. In work with adults, the analyst should be alert to intimations of the patient's significant other feeling threatened by the patient's increasing self-sufficiency. If the adult patient has not been helped to foster concomitant growth in the partner, the patient may suddenly feel faced with the choice of a summary ending of treatment or the rupture of a marriage. Because the adult patient may also have defensive reasons to avoid the various meanings of leaving, patient and partner may join forces to leave the analyst feeling abandoned, betrayed, and helpless.

> Dr. Y. was a highly successful professional who came to analysis profoundly depressed and frustrated with his personal and professional lives. He did not enjoy his work, his children, or his wife. He had been through many alternative treatments, from medication to meditation, with little relief. Psychoanalysis was a desperate last resort and he commuted an hour each way to attend a very early morning session time. This meant arising before 5 A.M., but he did this without complaint. At first this routine meshed with his sadomasochistic stance, the suffering that he felt entitled him to be cruel to his family.

In the middle phase of treatment he found more positive motivations for the deprivation consequent on his session time, as he began to enjoy his work, finding it stimulating and "endlessly fascinating." Treatment began to have a major impact on his lifelong passive, masochistic, victimized stance. He increasingly took charge of his own life and initiated major decisions, including ending his loveless marriage.

He began a relationship with a younger woman, whom he described as much less educated and sophisticated than he. After a year together he continued to describe her as someone who brought excitement, fun, and sexual pleasure to his life. Sometimes he slipped into his old sadomasochistic style of relating, but the analytic work had equipped him to counter this pull with assertion and realistic negotiation. Dr. Y. felt proud of his newfound capacity to take the initiative at home and at work. Both analyst and patient began to think of what work remained before starting a termination phase.

Then a shift occurred and the material became sparse; the pleasure and excitement in the analytic work seemed gone. For the first time in years, Dr. Y. overslept and began to complain about his commute and the need to wake up so early. Work on his conflicts about ending had some effect, but it was not consistent and did not feel very genuine. The analyst began to feel helpless as the treatment lost its vitality. The analyst questioned whether something was going on outside the treatment to produce such a change.

Dr. Y. then described that he had recently been involved in "nightly orgies" initiated by his girlfriend. They had gone far beyond their usual range of sexual activities. She had introduced a variety of sadomasochistic sexual practices, including role-playing, whipping, bondage, and spanking. Intuitively she had tapped into the patient's continuing battle between his closed-system sadomasochistic solutions to conflict and his hard-won open-system functioning. The patient said, "Doc, we've done great work together and I'm really grateful, but she has tapped into a side of me that I can't get away from. I'm hooked. It's a rush—like a drug. I can't wait to get home and I want to stay up all night playing our sexual games. I can't do both—I have to choose. I think we'll have to stop soon."

The analyst and the treatment could not compete with the rush of sexual excitement provided by Dr. Y.'s partner and how this interacted with his internal conflicts. Just like parents who cannot tolerate a child or adolescent's growth and the concomitant shifts in family dynamics, Dr. Y.'s partner seemed to fear she could not keep up if he kept on changing. Technically, the analyst had missed opportunities throughout the treatment to focus on Dr. Y.'s involvement of his partner in his progressive development.

In describing the work with Mark's father during the pretermination phase of Mark's treatment we noted his various difficulties in supporting and enjoying his son's growth. In that situation, there were two separate individuals, each with his own conflicts. If Mark and his father had not been involved in a treatment situation at the critical developmental juncture of Mark's late adolescence, Mark would have internalized some or all of his father's pathological reactions to his progressive changes. If Mark were then seen as an adult in individual treatment, it is likely that he would display serious resistance to change. The techniques we describe in working with parents of child patients can be used to illuminate difficulties, some reaching the dimensions of negative therapeutic reaction, in shifting adult patients from an exclusive reliance on omnipotent sadomasochistic, closed-system methods of self-regulation. What we see in work with parents of children and adolescents applies to the conflicts adult patients experience with internalized parent representations, particularly at moments of transition between phases of treatment.

The transition between the pretermination and termination phases is marked by agreement among child, analyst, and parents on a date for ending. After setting the date, child and parents enter with the analyst into the work of the termination phase. In the next paper we will describe parent work in the termination and posttermination phases.

References

Fonagy, P., Steele, M., Moran, G., et al. (1993). Measuring the ghost in the nursery: an empirical study of the relation between parents' mental representations of childhood experiences and their infants' security of attachment. *Journal of the American Psychoanalytic Association* 41: 957–989.

Furman, E. (1992). *Toddlers and Their Mothers.* Madison, CT: International Universities Press.

Heller, P. (1990). *A Child Analysis with Anna Freud.* Madison, CT: International Universities Press.

Novick, J. (1982). Termination: themes and issues. *Psychoanalytic Inquiry* 2:329–365.

——— (1990). Comments on termination in child, adolescent and adult analysis. *Psychoanalytic Study of the Child* 45:419–436. New Haven, CT: Yale University Press.

——— (1997). Termination conceivable and inconceivable. *Psychoanalytic Psychology* 14:145–162.

Novick, J., and Novick, K. K. (1991). Some comments on masochism and the delusion of omnipotence from a developmental perspective. *Journal of the American Psychoanalytic Association* 39:307–321.

——— (1994). Externalization as a pathological form of relating: the dynamic underpinning of abuse. In *Victims of Abuse: The Impact of Child and Adult Trauma*, ed. A. Sugarman, pp. 343–381. New York: International Universities Press.

——— (1996a). A developmental perspective on omnipotence. *Journal of Clinical Psychoanalysis* 5:129–173.

——— (1996b). *Fearful Symmetry*. Northvale, NJ: Aronson.

——— (2000). Love in the therapeutic alliance. *Journal of the American Psychoanalytic Association* 48:189–218.

——— (2001). Parent work in analysis—children, adolescents and adults. Part I—evaluation. *Journal of Infant, Child, and Adolescent Psychotherapy* 1:55–77.

——— (2002). Two systems of self-regulation. *Psychoanalytic Social Work* 8(3/4):95–122.

Novick, K. K., and Novick, J. (1998). An application of the concept of the therapeutic alliance to sadomasochistic pathology. *Journal of the American Psychoanalytic Association* 46:813–846.

——— (2002). Parent work in analysis II—children, adolescents and adults: recommendation, beginning and middle phases of treatment. *Journal of Infant, Child, and Adolescent Psychotherapy* 2(1):1–27.

JicaP Vol. 2, No. 2, 2002

Parent Work in Analysis: Children, Adolescents, and Adults. Part Four: Termination and Post-Termination Phases

Kerry Kelly Novick and Jack Novick, Ph.D.

Termination

Despite the spate of papers in the last thirty years on the topic of termination, the ending of treatment for adults and children remains an area of difficulty and conceptual controversy. This seems especially true in regard to termination work with parents. All too frequently, children and adolescents end treatment prematurely because of a unilateral decision on the part of their parents (Novick 1990). Our present focus on parent work derives from our experience that it is essential to a genuine completion of a child analysis that parents be an explicit part of the treatment plan throughout. Earlier papers in this series (J. Novick and K. K. Novick 2001, K. K. Novick and J. Novick 2002, this volume) have detailed conflicts, anxieties, and resistances that arise in parents and have suggested techniques for addressing them at each phase of treatment. Here we will look at issues in the termination phase and in the time after the therapy of the child or adolescent ends.

Termination of Parent Work

Assuming that there has been consistent work with parents throughout treatment, patient, parents, and analyst enter the termination phase with an agreed-upon ending date and a shared understanding of the tasks remaining to be accomplished. For the first time in the treatment, there is little danger of a premature, unilateral termination. But termination work with parents is crucial to helping them to support their child's adaptive use of the termination work, to meet the child's legitimate need for a supportive, validating other when the analyst is no longer available, and to foster their autonomous capacity to use the positive parenting skills they have developed. Another way to describe the task of parents during the termination phase is in terms of consolidation of the open-system functioning they have been able to achieve through the work of mastering the therapeutic alliance tasks of each phase of the treatment. The therapeutic alliance tasks for parents during termination are to allow the child to mourn and to internalize their relationship with the analyst in order to be able to carry on their parental development after treatment.

It is important for the analyst to acknowledge internally and explicitly that the parents and the therapist have a deep and significant bond. Saying goodbye to each other will evoke the complex feelings, anxieties, and defenses associated with separation and loss. This is true even if the parents and analyst have never actually met, for instance, when a late adolescent has been in treatment during college attendance at a distance. But they have all been part of an important effort together in the service of the patient's development and this creates a strong attachment. We say to parents that we adults need a goodbye time just as much as the child does; this is often particularly true for single parents, who have used the relationship with the child's therapist for support in their parental functioning.

Ordinary Parental Anxieties during Termination

At this time we listen for, and introduce if they are not forthcoming, parent questions about post-therapy contact. We try to detoxify the issue, that is, counteract any remaining fantasy idea of a relationship maintained by pain or pathology, by talking about their capacity to continue the work begun together through the therapy, how they now have the skills inside, as they have learned to listen differently and enlist their child in understanding and growing. We take up the magical, omnipotent belief that life can be trouble-free, and that therefore treatment should ensure a smooth passage, by introducing the idea that what they and their child have developed in treatment is "emotional muscle," a tolerance for ordinary stresses and strains. We also think through together how they will know if they have reached an impasse, or become stuck in trying to work on a problem. Here we point out that parents and analyst will always have a relationship, that the analyst is a lifelong resource. By exploring their feelings around potential future contact, remnants of guilt and shame may once more be addressed and the feeling of teamwork reinforced.

Resistance to Sadness

Just as the termination phase allows for a final reworking of core conflicts for the individual patient, so parents, faced with the reality of ending, often react with their characteristic anxieties and defenses. This was what we saw in the case of Tamara, who started a termination phase at 12, after two-and-a-half years of analysis.

> Throughout Tamara's treatment her parents had difficulty in allowing her psychological autonomy. This stemmed from intense anxiety about the power of Tamara's feelings, which in turn was based on a pathological belief in the omnipotence of feelings. The rigid suppression and control they had exercised to deal with this issue had largely disappeared by the time the decision to terminate was made jointly by child, parents, and analyst.
>
> As soon as the date was set, however, Tamara's mother became angry and depressed, like at the beginning of the treatment, and Tamara's father seemed helpless and discouraged, ineffectual in dealing with his own anger at his daughter and his wife. At the same time, some of the life seemed to go out of Tamara in her sessions. The analyst noted the similarity of this pattern to the beginning of the analysis and talked with the parents about all the changes that had taken place. In describing the hard work they had all done, the analyst remarked on how much they had gone through together, and how close this had made them all feel. Father then exclaimed, "Yes, it will really feel strange not to be coming here anymore." Mother sighed and frowned and said that it would be a relief, as then she could take Tamara to gymnastics. In the next week, mother continued to talk enthusiastically with Tamara about how much fun it was going to be when treatment ended. Both parents were struggling with their own conflicts about feelings, pushing away their good feelings about the analyst and the treatment for fear of sadness. But this also meant that they would then be unable to mourn their own loss, internalize the gains, and, importantly, absorb, tolerate, and support Tamara's mourning.
>
> The mother's reaction related to a central issue in her character. The analyst returned to the mother's shame at the impact of her rage and depression on her child, and the humiliation of having a child in treatment, longstanding themes in the parent work throughout. Tamara's mother cried as she described how much happier her daughter had become, and how badly she felt that her daughter had been so unhappy before. Here in the termination phase was the continuation of the transformation of guilt into usable concern that was begun at the evaluation. In the termination phase, some parents still struggle with achieving remorse that allows for reparation. The analyst addressed the magical assumption contained in the mother's guilt—that she should somehow be able to change the past—and suggested that the mother focus on the tools she now had available to ensure that the future would be different from the past.

> At the same time Tamara's father grappled with his defensive inhibition of feelings. When the analyst greeted his comment about how it would be when they didn't meet anymore with the acknowledgment, "Yes, we will miss each other," the father was able to own his good feelings for the work. He talked about how he and his wife had grown along with their daughter, and began to perceive the intensity of Tamara's feelings about the end of her treatment. When the analyst remarked that they might consider sharing their perceptions and feelings with their daughter, both parents smiled and said, "That will help us all!"

Tamara's parents needed to work during the termination period to tolerate their child's sadness and to acknowledge their own. Mourning is only possible when there are loving feelings, and internalization does not take place without mourning. Hence the critical importance of a good termination to the consolidation of therapeutic work and the parents' capacity to continue growing and fostering their child's growth subsequently.

Reworking of Core Conflicts and Generational Issues during Termination

In the previous papers in this series (Novick and Novick 2001, 2002) we have followed the course of parent work in conjunction with the treatment of Mark, the 22-year-old who had started treatment at 16 after nearly dying from a suicide attempt.

> At the start of his analysis Mark, like his father, had a very limited range of emotional experience or expression. Through the generations, the men in his family took pride in their ability to withstand harrowing physical or psychological assault without displaying any feeling. Mark had outbursts of rage or moments of sadistic glee when he bested an opponent. Any other feeling, such as love, sadness, or sympathy, was considered counterproductive and a sign of weakness.
>
> By the end of treatment both father and son had an alternative to the family ideal of macho mercenary men kept in check only by dominating women. Mark changed sooner and more extensively; he also had greater certainty that being a loving, caring, feeling man was preferable to being a sadistic, cold, emotionally dead person. During the course of the parent work Mark's father had also extended his range of feelings, but this new way of being was limited to his relationship with his son. Given the father's own history of multiple losses and separations, it was not surprising that he

reacted to the termination decision with his longstanding character armor of emotional withdrawal.

Mark's father was cordial, correct, and distracted in parent sessions as the 14-week countdown to termination began. He no longer seemed to feel any concern about Mark's capacity to maintain his positive changes. In a turnaround from his earlier worry that it might be rushing things to consider termination, once the date was set, he wondered if a three-month ending period was needlessly prolonging the goodbye. "As far as I'm concerned, there's nothing more to work on. I won't interfere with your work with Mark, but our work on my parenting issues and my relationship with my son seems to have reached an end. My son and I are getting along well—we enjoy and respect each other. I'm glad. I'm grateful. But I think we can stop now."

The analyst agreed that father and son had come a long way, but pointed out that termination is a time of consolidation. Mark was doing that in his treatment and it might be helpful to the father to do the same, to go over what they had learned together, and thus ensure that the positive changes could become a permanent part of the father's personality. Mark's father saw the logic in that and agreed to continue through Mark's termination phase.

The analyst focused mainly on the changes in the range of father's feelings toward Mark, how father could now experience and express love, sadness, remorse, and worry. In the context of the family tradition of toughness, such changes were even more impressive and remarkable, a praiseworthy product of very hard work. Then the analyst spoke of Mark's struggle to extend this open-system way of relating to all his relationships, beyond those he considered safe, like his father and brother. Mark had discovered that he was far less vulnerable and more in realistic control if he let himself feel the full range of feelings in any relationship. He did this, the analyst said, by practicing in his therapy, allowing himself to know and express love, sadness, hurt, anger, disappointment, pride, and so forth. This allowed Mark to find pleasure at work and a meaningful relationship with both his parents.

Father added his perception of the change in Mark's dating pattern, in his making a more permanent relationship with a very nice person. "But," he said, "this is another area where Mark has gone beyond me. I don't think I ever loved anyone until my children were born and then I didn't know how to love them. Here, with you, I've learned that it's good to be able to feel and express my love for them. But I'm the same cold, unfeeling prick with everyone else, including my wife."

The analyst took up this perception, noting that it was a considerable achievement to be able to tolerate and enjoy differences in skills, styles of thinking, accomplishments, and so forth. However, differences in self-protective emotional stances often create tensions in relationships. Without realizing it consciously, Mark and his father might each feel threatened by their different ways of dealing with feelings, and that could naturally lead to retreating from each other. Father wondered what to do about it. The analyst suggested that father, like Mark, could practice these skills in the safe setting of the parent work relationship, with the current task of saying goodbye. As this was the end of a very long and important relationship, perhaps he could allow himself to feel and express his feelings. As tears came to the father's eyes, the analyst added that this was indeed a meaningful relationship for them both, and that Mark and his father would be very much missed.

Mark's father associated to his own memory from when he was 3 years old of his father's departure for wartime service. He had cried and his parents had told him he was a little soldier and brave soldiers don't cry, that if he had to cry like a little baby, he should go to his room. He recalled taking deep breaths, telling himself not to cry, and then feeling very grown up and proud when praised by his parents. His father was killed a year later, and, again, he felt proud for not crying, for being a brave little soldier.

Mark's mother had dropped out of the direct parent work during the middle phase of Mark's analysis, as she had felt too threatened by the prospect of addressing her responsibility for Mark's abused childhood. She had, however, continued to work at a distance, making use of what her husband brought back from parent sessions and changing in her interactions with Mark. The analyst invited her to come back to parent sessions to say goodbye. She attended a couple of times and expressed her sense that the whole family had gained a tremendous amount from the years of work together. Parent work with Mark's mother had some impact, but the limitations were also clear, in that her character was constructed on the basis of externalizations that she could not relinquish.

In the last seven weeks of the termination period, in the context of his sadness at saying goodbye, Mark's father went over the positive changes in his parenting, especially his newfound capacity to respect and enjoy his son's separate existence. With his practicing feeling a fuller range of affects also came some negative feelings of disillusionment and disappointment in the analyst and the process. In particular, both Mark and his father had to come to terms with their feelings about the fact that what we have termed "closed-system sadomasochistic functioning" was still present and available. It had not been eradicated, only decreased in intensity and contained by alternative open-system possibilities. They would both have to continue working after analysis to address conflicts between these alternative ways to regulate themselves and resolve conflicts. But they were equipped with the capacities gained in the course of mastering the therapeutic alliance tasks during each phase of treatment. Father and Mark could then imagine the post-analytic phase realistically, sensitive to signs of reverting to closed-system functioning and aware of being equipped to deal with these conflicts. This included the knowledge they could contact the analyst at any time if they needed or wanted to.

There are some parents who are not ready to finish the work with the therapist, who continue to struggle with the tasks of parenthood and allowing the child a separate existence. This problem may appear in the form of reluctance to allow the child to finish, with apparently extreme anxiety about their or the child's ability to cope without the therapist. When this difficulty has appeared during the pre-termination phase, we sometimes delay the termination decision to allow parents time to catch up. If they have seemed to do well with the decision to terminate and the anxiety escalates only during termination, it may be an acute reaction to separation. Often, acknowledgment of the importance of the relationship, the sadness of ending, and verbalizing the fearful belief that the end will be like death is sufficient. Sometimes, however, extreme parental anxiety during the termination phase has different implications.

SEVERE PATHOLOGY IN PARENTS

In the paper on beginning the treatment (K. K. Novick and J. Novick 2002) we noted that the parents of child and adolescent patients that we see are often more disturbed than individual adults who seek treatment for themselves. Like Mark's mother, they may deny all responsibility for any psychological problems. Blame and responsibility are externalized and the idea of individual therapy is too threatening to even consider.

Some tolerate parent work throughout the child's treatment, apply what is worked on, and show great gains. But, as termination approaches, it becomes clear that they cannot internalize and consolidate what they have learned. It seems as if the parental ego and superego in these situations is dependent on the presence of the analyst. Parents with these difficulties will not be able to support their children in maintaining the progressive momentum regained through analysis. In these cases we explore the possibility of continuing to work with the parents after the end of the child's treatment. Then we must work carefully with the child to discover his or her feelings about this; we describe that the work with the parents will not be about the child, but rather to help them with some of the difficulties they have as parents, none of which is unfamiliar to the child. When this structure is really needed, most children are relieved to know that their parents will have the therapist available. The realities and limitations of this relationship as a conduit from the child to the analyst are explored in relation to the child's various fantasies about continuing contact. Then we continue to see the parent or parents, with the additional goal of making a referral for individual treatment, so that they can address the personality difficulties that hold them back from open-system functioning and growth as parents.

Post-Termination

The time after finishing cannot strictly be considered a phase of treatment, yet all the preceding work has been aimed at enhancing later functioning in parents and children, and a specific goal of treatment has been to equip them to continue working and growing on their own. There is a growing literature on post-termination in individual treatments of adults, but very little about this phase in child and adolescent patients and nothing about parents. This is another juncture where we have found our conceptualization of phase-specific therapeutic alliance tasks useful, both in setting criteria for moving into a termination phase and defining the goals. This leads in turn to understanding criteria and goals in relation to the time after treatment. We talk with patients and their parents during the termination phase about the tasks of post-analytic living. In particular we focus on the inevitable disappointments of life; the necessity for continued work, internally and in their relationships; and the type of post-analytic contact appropriate to the continuing analytic relationship. During termination we discuss how they will feel when they experience disillusionment and disappointment with the analyst and the analysis, what it will be like when they surpass the analyst's understanding in their independent work. We raise these issues for parents to think about so that they will not be surprised later. Then the gains of treatment are more likely to be maintained.

Varieties of Post-Treatment Contact with Parents

Despite the difficulties that can arise in cases of severe parental pathology, most parents are ready to finish work at the same time as their children. Indeed, this synchrony is one measure of the renewal of closeness at a new level in the parent–child relationship. There is a whole spectrum of ways that parents in our experience have used the opportunity of post-analytic contact. Sometimes we never hear from a family again after termination. These have usually been cases in which we have done a minimum of parent work.

CONSULTING THE ANALYST

When we have worked consistently with parents, one common pattern is to hear from them when some big decision faces the family. It is not so much that they seek advice or help, rather it is a form of consultation, as with the parents of Felicia, who had been in therapy for unhappiness and somnambulism from ages 8 to 10.

> Felicia had worked very effectively to address her highly anxious, perfectionistic, and demanding relationship with herself and her parents. Her harsh internal standards had intersected with a number of untimely deaths in her immediate circle, which had exacerbated her troubles. Once she was in therapy, her symptoms abated and she was eventually able to enjoy school and friends in new, dependable ways. Her parents had both faithfully attended parent sessions through which they came to develop greater insight into their little girl's ways of thinking and to respect her feelings, while retaining their parental authority. Everyone felt it had been a very successful treatment.
>
> Eight months after termination, the parent of one of Felicia's classmates died suddenly. The parents called the analyst to talk about their handling of this news and their plans about funeral attendance and so forth. Their call was in the nature of "running it by the analyst." The analyst thought they had made very good use of their gains from treatment, making wise decisions and speaking sensitively and sensibly with their daughter. These parents had learned how to think about what was meaningful to Felicia, how to stay with her, how to communicate, and how to value their importance in helping their daughter through the sometimes hard vagaries of life.

NEWS

Occasionally a parent shows great empathy during the termination phase for the analyst's loss when treatment finishes. This seems to be due to the analyst's having succeeded in reassuring the parent of his or her primacy with the child. These are parents who then feel they can securely share the child with the analyst, as we saw with Kyla's mother.

> Kyla started treatment as a violently aggressive preschooler and finished successfully at the age of 7. Much of the parent work addressed the parents' valuing of themselves and how to help their child with loyalty conflicts between their very different parenting styles.
>
> Several months after the end of therapy, Kyla's mother phoned the analyst "because I knew you would so appreciate this." She described coming home from work and snapping angrily at Kyla. Later she apologized, and explained to the child in some detail about her sense that she was taking something out on Kyla that really belonged in another situation. Uncertain about whether this concept was getting across, she asked Kyla, only to be met with a big grin and the remark, "Of course I understand how people sometimes do that. Why do you think I went to my analyst for so long?"

NEGOTIATING DEVELOPMENTAL TRANSITIONS

A potential difficulty for families is their child's passage from one developmental phase to the next. Throughout the work with parents we try to anticipate the issues these transitions may bring in the future, noting parents' problematic reactions to phase changes during treatment and the meanings ascribed to them, often as losses or separations. We talk to parents about what to expect in latency or adolescence, and how to monitor their own reactions. Post-treatment contact is often initiated by parents at these moments, as we saw repeatedly in the case of Christina, who met with her therapist intermittently over fifteen years.

> Christina's parents had divorced acrimoniously when she was a toddler, but had agreed on joint custody. The course of their arrangements never ran smoothly, but the different sets of parents/stepparents had each come to separate parent sessions throughout Christina's treatment during her preschool and latency years. In that work they had become able to agree to disagree about their parenting, but to put their child's needs above their own wish to triumph over each other.
>
> Each time Christina entered a new phase, however, all four parents seemed to struggle to stay securely ensconced in the phase of parenthood. Old defensive patterns of relating with each other and with Christina flared up and interfered with Christina's progressive development. Christina found her parents impossibly demanding and rigid, and the parents were at log-

gerheads. Each time, at the entrance to middle school, to high school, and to college, Christina asked to see the analyst. After two sessions on each of these occasions, it became clear that Christina was doing well, maintaining her progressive development, but that it was threatened by her parents' pathology. The analyst met jointly with Christina and all four parents to talk through the practical issues that they were having such trouble about. Although the sessions focused on discussing concrete problems, like school choice or use of a car, the process and the presence of the analyst seemed to reestablish the parents in the phase of parenthood they had achieved earlier.

RETURN TO TREATMENT

An important measure of the solidity and depth of parent work in a child or adolescent treatment is the parents' capacity to return without shame, guilt, or reproach to see the analyst when they are concerned that their child is running into difficulties. Sometimes a few sessions of parent work can resolve the worry if it springs from a parental reaction to developmental shifts, as we saw from Christina's situation, or from disagreement between parents, who simply need a setting in which to talk the issue through.

Sometimes, however, parents have accurately perceived that their child is foundering in the face of new challenges from development or outside circumstances. When the child or adolescent reenters treatment the parent work can proceed on the foundation of the strong positive working relationship established in the first treatment. Parents and analyst know each other very well and the work is efficient and deep at the same time.

LONG-TERM FOLLOW-UP

One criterion for self-monitoring that we discuss with both patient and parents during the termination phase is the nature of the internal image they carry of the analyst after finishing.

> Jane had ended her analysis at 21 after five years of work. Work with her parents ended at the same time. In the four or five years afterward, the analyst received occasional notes from Jane about important developments—her marriage, her first publication, the births of her children. There was no news for twelve years when Jane called the analyst for an appointment, saying that she had fallen into a terrible, suicidal depression like before she began treatment. When she was feeling hopeless, her mother had reminded her of how the analyst had talked about monitoring her internal images.

> When Jane saw that she had lost her sense of the analyst as a benign, loving resource she realized that she was killing off something important inside herself, and that this was a real danger signal. Jane and her mother were able to use tools from the treatment long before to deal with a current crisis.

Work with parents can lead to a deep, unforgettable experience for all parties, as we saw with Jane's mother, who kept the image of Jane's analyst alive inside even when Jane could not. A last example comes from the treatment of Robert, who began analysis at 3 with a diagnosis of atypical or autistic development and ended treatment at 7 years of age.

> Robert's treatment had ended 30 years earlier. The analyst had relocated and had not heard from the family since. Robert's family saw a notice of a conference at the center where he had been treated, with the analyst's name featured as a speaker. Robert's mother left the following letter:
>
> ". . . The reason I wanted to write to you for so long was to say that things have turned out so well for Robert." She described his school career, with success in academics and with friends, and his constructive and explorative adolescence. "He loved university where he also met his future wife." She said he had done very well and pursued a career as a professional. "He has plenty of work, is very good at it and loves it. He is happily married with 2 children. He is an exceptionally gifted and good father, as well as an excellent cook! He stands six foot four inches, is very serious and occasionally tense. He is very self-aware and totally honest about himself, he is affectionate and able to express his feelings. I think he is happy on the whole.
>
> "I thought you'd like to know about him, because you made a great contribution to his development by encouraging him to come out of his confines.
>
> "Lastly I wanted to say that I too benefited from my visits to see you during a pretty difficult period in my life. For all this many thanks."

Application to Individual Work with Adults

The significant other of the adult patient, like the parent of a child in treatment, has had a long, complex, meaningful relationship with the analyst, even though they usually never meet and it is mediated through the patient. Just as the child analyst is aware that the parent needs to mark the end of the relationship and be helped to mourn, the analyst of the adult has to help that patient see how the ending will impact the significant other. The spouse or other person needs to have his or her feelings acknowledged, both for that individual's growth, and to be able to support the patient's mourning. Like the actual parent of the child patient, the adult's partner has to acknowledge and work through feelings of disappointment and disillusionment. Only by recognizing the reality limitations of treatment will the partner be able to accept the fact that the work will continue without the analyst. Finally, just as parents increasingly take on the parental functions initially shared by the analyst, such as validating, appreciating, admiring, and so forth, so the significant other has to be there for the adult patient so that basic human needs can be gratified in a realistic, open, mutual relationship.

References

Novick, J. (1990). Comments on termination in child, adolescent and adult analysis. *Psychoanalytic Study of the Child* 45:419–436. New Haven, CT: Yale University Press.

Novick, J., and Novick, K. K. (2001). Parent work in analysis: children, adolescents, and adults. Part I: the evaluation phase. *Journal of Infant, Child, and Adolescent Psychotherapy* 1:55–77.

——— (2002). Parent work in analysis: children, adolescents, and adults. Part III: middle and pretermination phases of treatment. *Journal of Infant, Child, and Adolescent Psychotherapy* (this volume).

Novick, K. K., and Novick, J. (2002). Parent work in analysis: children, adolescents, and adults. Part II: recommendation, beginning, and middle phases of treatment. *Journal of Infant, Child, and Adolescent Psychotherapy* 2(1):1–27.

JicaP Vol. 2, No. 2, 2002

Locating the Metaphor and Sensing the Poetic: Psychotherapy with Children in States of Nonexperiencing

Ionas Sapountzis, Ph.D.

There have been many articles in the psychoanalytic literature describing the difficulties in working with very withdrawn and disengaged patients, with patients who seem cut off from the world and have ceased to process their experiences. Psychoanalysts have used terms like "psychic deadness" (Eigen 1996), state of "non-experience" (Ogden 1989), state of "foreclosure" (McDougall 1984) and "psychic retreat" (Steiner 1993) to describe adult patients who experience themselves in various degrees of isolation and disengagement in life. The withdrawal from life and disengagement that these patients experience is not temporary or transient, but is a more entrenched and stable feature in their way of being in the world. Their "deadness," their "retreat" from contact, their nonexperiencing, all represent attempts to avoid internal and external pressures, to stay out of contact from a persecutory and fragmenting reality and to maintain a sense of safety, however fragile and ineffective.

According to Steiner (1993) the disengagement that patients experience can be expressed in multiple ways, depending on the patient's personality organization and history. Patients can seek safety either through a very aloof and schizoid type of distancing, through fleeing from contact due to intense anxiety, through contemptuous dismissal and narcissistic superiority, or even through a type of false and superficial engagement. Whatever the particular mode of disengagement, the bottom line is that such patients seek relief and safety in withdrawing and avoiding contact with reality.

In working with such patients, the therapist has to be able to tolerate and process the paralysis that is experienced in the room, the feeling that the treatment is unsuccessful, that he or she is failing as a therapist. The deadness, the paralysis that is enacted in the room often feels palpable, and in the countertransference the therapist is likely to feel intrusive and forceful or avoidant and passive. Though several writers (Alvarez 1992, Newirth 1996, Tustin 1984, 1986) have stressed the importance for the therapist who works with patients with autistic or schizoid types of pathological organization to actively intervene in order to avoid being rendered ineffective and/or to collude with the patient's pathology, others have made different arguments. Balint (1968), Josephs (1983), and Steiner (1993) have all concluded that very anxious and poorly organized patients can experience the therapist's comments and interpretations as too threatening and fragmenting. Balint (1968) believes that the therapist needs to provide patients who are functioning at the level of the basic fault with an experience and an object that is not "too sharply contoured." Josephs (1983) has observed that many borderline, highly anxious patients seek in therapy the experience and comfort of being understood and show little interest—if not outright resistance—in understanding themselves. In discussing therapeutic interventions with patients in a state of retreat and severe pathological organization, Steiner (1993) made the distinction between analyst-based and patient-based interpretations. Steiner argues that the latter are seen as more intrusive and confrontational and therefore are better suited after some level of trust and integration has been established.

Despite their paralysis and fears, despite their disengagement, adult patients, by virtue of coming to therapy, acknowledge their impasse and their need to connect, to link, and to feel alive. In seeking therapy, they express, however mutely, their desire and hope to connect, and the task for the therapist is to expand upon this timid gesture, to facilitate communication, and to establish a working alliance. For very frightened and disengaged children, however, being in therapy does not represent hope and promise, but defeat and confirmation of a persecutory reality. Unlike adult patients, who often seek a sense of comfort and the experience of being understood, children in retreat try to desperately avoid a persecutory world and the realization of their own "badness." They are in a state of retreat and disengagement to shield themselves from a painful external reality and to preserve whatever fragments of individuality and uniqueness they have from psychic annihilation and depersonalization. The paralysis and terror that they project in the therapy room is often associated with the experience of a painful loss that has left them numb and frozen in the face of their own separateness and aloneness. The loss of the good object that these children have experienced in their lives leaves them in a terrifying state from which they need to retreat.

In this paper, the cases of two young adolescents, in states of disconnectedness and isolation, are presented. Both patients conveyed a sense of vacancy and resignation, and contact was very difficult to initiate. It will be argued that it is not enough to contain or interpret their projections or lack thereof. As Alvarez (1992) points out, the feeling that is created in the countertransference may have less to do with the child's projections and more to do with the lack of such projections. The therapist not only has to create "a" feeling as Alvarez suggests, but has to get himself in touch with a feeling in order to be able to connect. Because of the deadness in the room, because of the fear and the paralysis, the therapist has to reach deep into his own reverie, into his subjective states, in order to understand the patient's projections, and to be able to find a language to communicate.

The Case of Lena

The need to help withdrawn children get in touch with "a" feeling and to create an experience was strongly felt with Lena, a 12-year-old girl who came for therapy a year after the death of her mother. A lively and demanding girl before her mother's illness, she now sat immobile and emotionless, her jacket zipped up to her neck despite the room's comfortable temperature, hands clasped over her knees, avoiding eye contact and ignoring my presence. Her joyless demeanor was an attempt to muffle her reality, to mask the terrifying loss she had experienced, and to keep her internal world at bay. She seemed convinced that there was nothing in the world for her to take in, and did not seem to expect anything from anyone. At home, Lena was left alone to mourn her mother's death. Her father had been unable to address her sense of loss and he himself had retreated behind a busy schedule. The main selfobject tie (Stolorow and Atwood 1992) between Lena and her father was her performance in school. She excelled in school, was the recipient of several academic awards, and was placed in a gifted class, recognitions and achievements that she dismissed with a shrug of her shoulders. She had become increasingly withdrawn from her peers and from social activities and spent the weekends taking care of her pets, cleaning their cages, and rearranging the furniture in her room, repetitive acts that served to create the illusion of being cared for and caring. Ogden (1989) describes these rhythmic acts as "sensation thoughts" (p. 54) in the absence of subjectivity, and views them as experiences that serve to replace the sensation and reliability that is missing in the patient's object world.

To understand the child, to decipher meaning, therapists usually rely on the child's play. The child's play is treated as a symbolic act, which—however disorganized—means something, reveals the child's unconscious life. Even chaotic play, play that is full of explosive acts and impulsive reactions, is used to develop meaning and is considered to reflect the child's internal state, the child's experience in and understanding of the world. Facilitating the child's ability to play and to develop a coherent play narrative is regarded by Slade (1994) as a needed step in helping children to create meaning and to feel their acts as meaningful and purposeful. With poorly organized, impulsive children, Slade believes that the emphasis should be on encouraging them to play, and on helping them to develop a meaningful context and a coherent narrative, rather than on interpreting their conflicts and unconscious motives. From an ego-psychoanalytical perspective, the therapist's role is to strengthen the child's ego, the child's sense of mastery and coherence, before attempting interpretations that amplify the child's insecurity and sense of lack of control. At the opposite end of the pole, Kleinians believe that by interpreting the child's conflict first, the anxiety will be removed or lessened, and the child will become more accessible. Whatever the theoretical orientation, whichever way the treatment is conceptualized, the therapist is faced with the task of helping the child to develop a narrative and to build a more coherent and better integrated sense of self. Children in a state of psychic retreat though, do not act out their impulses and fears, nor do they express their conflicts through symbolic acts, whether externalized or internalized. Having withdrawn from a painful reality, being removed from contact and experiencing, they are likely to remain distant and distrustful of any attempt by the therapist to convey or construct meaning. Unlike children who see the therapist as a container, who rely on the therapist, children in a state of psychic retreat do not seek contact nor continuity. The prospect of being "met" or "found" is not only unfathomable but also unsettling.

Lena appeared indifferent to everything in the room and ignored my comments and attempts to verbally engage with her. It was easy to feel lacking and irrelevant in the countertransference, just as the world felt lacking and irrelevant to her. In the matrix of inadequacy and hopelessness that was enacted in the room, I felt thwarted and ineffective and found it hard not to seek refuge in the safety of repetitive and rhythmic acts, like board games, or to react to the feeling of passivity by becoming intrusive and concrete. Tustin (1972) had urged therapists to avoid being rendered "null and void" in therapy, and to try instead to pierce the child's autistic shell. This, however, is more the case with autistic children who are absorbed into their encapsulated selves and appear oblivious to the world. For Lena, the opposite was the case. Having experienced an almost adhesive identification (Meltzer 1975) with her mother, she was now at a complete loss, frozen in her absence, emotionally adrift and vacant. She had not withdrawn to an autistic or self-centered state in which the outside world was foreclosed, but to an empty, self-less inner world, a state of nonexperience, of suspended existence in which she did not have to process or acknowledge the pain over the loss of her mother. Removed from any type of subjective awareness and self-experiencing, she existed in an objectified world, in a reality that was defined by external rules and rituals of engagement, which gave her an illusive sense of purpose and definition.

Drawing attention to her mode of engagement or to her emotional state, however sensitively or playfully done, was experienced as a direct threat, as an attack. Slade (1994) argues that with acting-out or impulsive children, the language has to first become what Piaget has called, a system of "signifiers," which is a system of symbolic signs that is disconnected from bodily and primitive impulses. Language has to become independent of primitive, narcissistic ties in order for the therapist's interpretations and verbal statements to be processed. Unlike the children in various stages of disorganization that Slade writes about, children in a state of retreat have no difficulty separating and processing verbal statements. Their language has become a system of "signifiers," a system that they use effectively to process and convey an "objectified" external reality. But when it comes to their subjective, inner reality, this language is transformed from an objectified to a persecutory system of signifiers. Relying on language to convey meaning, to reassure or explore, does not make them feel connected. Attempts to interpret or bring to their attention aspects of their behavior are experienced as intrusive and fragmenting and intensify their perception of the world as a persecutory place. For these children, their subjective and intersubjective experiences are feared, and are treated as beta-elements that cannot be processed and have to be evacuated (Bion 1963). Winnicott (1971a) argues that with patients who do not experience the therapeutic encounter as an unfolding, meaningful process, patients who "cannot play," the therapist's interpretations and verbal elaborations are often perceived as confusing and irrelevant. The challenge is not how or whether to interpret the conflict or how to address the deficit, but how to detoxify meaning, how to make children less frightened of their reality and subjective states. With children who feel isolated and disengaged from the world, the task becomes how to create, capture, and encourage moments in which they feel more alive, more accessible to experiencing. To create a link between their symbolic acts and subjective experiences, to amplify the meaning of their acts, the therapist needs to make his presence felt, needs to become a "live company" (Alvarez 1992), needs to help create a new experience.

After a couple of awkward, stilted sessions, Lena resorted to filling up her time by drawing intersecting lines on a page and then using colored crayons to fill the spaces inside. It was her first attempt to fill the vacuum in the session, her first act of communication, however distant and self-absorbed it appeared, and conveyed the aimlessness and meaninglessness in her life, as well as the fragmenting experiences and the empty spaces inside her that she needed to fill. To preserve and amplify Lena's first creative act, her first attempt at symbolization, I introduced the Squiggle game. I was surprised by the quality of her drawings, by her ease and ability to express in the metaphor the emptiness in her life. Her drawings, it became clear to me, captured eloquently her psychic state, her psychic reality, her longing to be picked up, to feel connected. I was surprised at how close they were to her reality, a reality that she could not articulate with words. Her squiggles became a safe way to express and articulate her loneliness without having to face how alone and abandoned she felt in the world. Gradually, the themes of her squiggles began to shift from her conscious affective need to be held and acknowledged to her experience of the loss of her mother and her terrible loneliness. She drew black holes in space, little figures utterly alone in their environment, and empty roads leading nowhere. She drew in silence and I became more silent, in order to respect her need for privacy in the presence of an adult.

The act of playing, according to Winnicott (1971a), implies trust and belongs to the potential space between the child and the parent. Children in a state of retreat have lost their capacity or better, their desire, to play. Fearful of contact, distrustful of their environment, they can neither process nor symbolize their experiences. Being playful and spontaneous in the absence of a facilitating object and an experiencing self is an impossible act.

Winnicott (1971a) equates play and the capacity to play with the experience of being creative and alive. The role of the therapist, therefore, is to allow and enable the patient to play, to facilitate the patient's capacity to feel creative and be creative. If the therapist cannot facilitate a playful exchange, cannot create a playful interaction, then, according to Winnicott (1971a), "he is not suitable for the work" (p. 54). In my experience, children in a state of retreat have been deprived of a mirroring experience, of the flow of exchange with their parents, the give and take that leads a person to experience himself as an emerging entity, as an emerging individual. Deprived of mutual and validating exchanges, they are rooted in a concrete world where spontaneity, individualism, and creativity are ignored and discouraged, and in their place, compliance, acquiescence, and obedience—in short, a paranoid existence—is fostered. To develop a sense of trust, to feel less persecuted, they need to feel noticed and attended to in therapy; they need to feel that every trace, every flicker of a response, is met and valued. For Winnicott (1971a) psychotherapy has to be a spontaneous and liberating experience of playing and not just a series of interpretations. In an often quoted statement, Winnicott goes as far as to state that "if the patient cannot play, then something needs to be done to enable the patient to become able to play, after which psychotherapy may begin" (1971a, p. 54). Lena's response to the squiggle lines and her drawings were spontaneous and creative acts and reflected a growing trust in expressing and conveying her reality in the presence of an adult.

As Lena's drawings accumulated, it became clear that they not only articulated her psychic reality and her experiences, but were also helping her to process and mourn her mother's death. She was mourning in a silent, detached manner and could not reflect or comment on her drawings. Yet, her silence felt less dissociative and she seemed less detached. Instead, it felt more anchored to her experience, more in tune with her grief and loneliness. She continued to draw tiny figures and empty spaces but was also drawing personal objects that were lost or remained unclaimed by their owner. I commented that these were beautiful drawings that to me "spoke" about loneliness and about people who had moved on and were missed. She transformed her next two squiggles into broken hearts and a tornado in space.

Lena continued to draw, always in silence, and gradually seemed more engaging and engaged afterwards. She became increasingly more affective in the room, started responding to my queries, and began seeking other activities to do. Her drawings, though still devoid of people, reflected a warming attitude, a tendency to be more caring and present in her creative acts.

In her book *Live Company*, Alvarez (1992) gives a wonderful description of a colleague's (Miss N.) effort to locate and amplify the experience of a very primitive child. To quote from her: "Sometimes, all Cindy would do was to open her mouth slightly and Miss N. would say 'I think you want to say something.' It was not always clear that Cindy had intended to say anything" (p. 100).

With Lena, one could not make such a statement. It was too direct, too threatening. It implied agency and a reality that she could not tolerate. Instead, she needed the initiative of a squiggly line to become engaged and to begin processing her mother's loss without having to articulate it with words. My role was to stay as discreetly present as possible, to facilitate without making her feel pushed. Statements became evocative commentaries on her drawings, deliberately opaque and vague. While attempting to discreetly make myself present to her, I was also trying to evoke in her a theme, a link, a preconception (Bion 1963). In the transitional space of the Squiggle game, Lena was able to express the unthinkable and acknowledge her longing through her symbols. The loss of her mother, though still a deeply painful experience, was less deadening. She was now beginning to experience a sense of purpose and to acknowledge the presence of other objects and her need for them.

In our session prior to the summer break, she transformed the last squiggle into a hand on a doorknob "opening or closing the door" as she put it. Her drawing was both a greeting and a goodbye, and captured perfectly the changes in her psychic reality, as well as our shared experience. It felt even more poignantly in touch with our reality when after the summer, citing a busy schedule and despite Lena's preferences and my recommendations, her father informed me that she would not be able to continue with her treatment. Over the summer Lena had become more involved with social activities and had enrolled in a theater group. Her grandmother expressed her surprise at how much more active Lena seemed to her, in seeking out contact and stating what she wanted. In the context of these developments, Lena's last squiggle also symbolized her opening up, her ability to put her hand on the doorknob and to step out into the world.

THE CASE OF DAVID

David, a 15-year-old bright adolescent, with a history of school refusal, insomnia, and depressed affect, presented a very different picture. Angry and distant, he sat on the edge of the couch, hands hanging over his knees, waiting for me to make a statement, to create meaning and comfort, yet convinced of the uselessness of it all. Over the past six or seven years, David's relationships with his family had become so tempestuous that he had to leave his house and move in with his aunt. He did not have many friends and spent most of his time in front of his computer. He would typically stay up until late into the night, browsing the Internet, creating and recreating web pages, and sending email messages to electronic "friends" around the world. Getting up in the morning was a prolonged battle and he often spent the rest of his day feeling sleepy and irritable. Unlike Lena, who had retreated into a state of nonexistence, David—feeling rejected and cast out—had retreated into an isolated existence, into a state of being that was full of rage and bitterness.

I had the image of an orphan boy who, in a moment of defiance and misplaced pride, had expressed that he did not want to live home anymore and his parents had replied "fine." He felt "dropped" and projected his sense of failure and rage outward, leaving him in a state of vacuum and making any exchange very difficult. Confined to a state of bitter isolation, he kept deflecting any kind of subjective awareness, and retreated into an insulated existence.

The sessions felt rigid and stale, more or less a straightforward representation of David's internal object relationships. Unlike Lena, David did not avoid a conversation or recoil at a topic; rather, he "dropped" all my attempts to have a conversation, to have a meaningful contact. He did not try to avoid my gaze; instead, he kept staring in my direction with cold, even contemptuous, detachment. His arrogant and dismissive style served to avoid the internal chaos and confusion that he was experiencing. In treating all attempts at engagement as nothing, as irrelevant, he not only projected out the feeling of his own irrelevance, but also protected himself from noticing and from his fear of being noticed. Being in therapy made him feel very anxious and threatened his precarious equilibrium. He was in therapy because of his badness, because he "needed" therapy, and that sensation was tapping into his experience of being "dropped," of people dismissing him. He felt so splintered and disintegrated, his object world so unbearable, that as a defense he had adopted an omnipotent organization of contemptuous superiority. In the transference illusion, I had become the persecutory, rejecting, and dismissing parent and he could not tolerate that. Interpretations or observing comments, no matter how supportively conveyed, were experienced as intrusions, as "things in themselves" (Bion 1957), that threatened to deprive him of the protection of his retreat. He could not be engaged in the here and now, or in the past or future.

Ekstein (1983a,b) believes that to approach children who are difficult to reach, the therapist has to participate and interpret within the child's metaphor in order to remain within the child's mythology. He cautions therapists never to attack the role or identity a child has chosen in his play, never to impose a quality of insight that the child cannot accept or comprehend. This is the case for children who live in a fluid landscape, full of outer spaces, mythical encounters, fictional creatures, and timelessness, the "time and space" children that Ekstein has written so much about. It is also very much the case for withdrawn and frozen children like Lena and David, who live in a barren landscape where the past and the future are not connected to the present, where physical presence does not correspond to actually being present, where the "I" is dissociated from the "me," and life is lived in a suspended vacuum. To become self-conscious, to be able to represent, process, and transform his own experiences, an individual will have to construct his own symbols and metaphors. Ogden (1997a) believes that the language used between the patient and the therapist has to reflect the experience of being alive. If the language of the therapist or patient becomes stagnant, it fails to convey the sense of a living human experience, the sense of a meaningful relationship. In therapy with children in a state of retreat, one has to find the language that makes the interaction feel alive. Alvarez (1992) emphasizes again and again the need to create a feeling, "any" feeling, with autistic children.

With David, the issue was not how to create or stir a feeling in him, but how to find a place to connect, how to find a language that made him feel valued and present. I believe that this is as important for the patient who experiences himself as utterly cut off and disliked as it is for the therapist who, because of the projected deadness and destructiveness, needs to feel moved and engaged, needs to find reasons to be hopeful and alive, and to convey that in the room. Without developing and relying on his own metaphors and symbolisms, his own subjective experiences, the therapist, Ogden (1997a) points out, runs the risk of finding himself "stuck in a world of surfaces with meanings that cannot be reflected upon" (p. 727).

In a recent interview, José Saramago, the Portuguese novelist and 1998 Nobel laureate, described a scene from his childhood that made an indelible impression on him. He remembers witnessing his grandfather, an illiterate and rather reticent peasant, who, right before leaving for Lisbon to be treated for a serious illness, went out in the fields, hugged the trees he had planted, and cried. To the 5-year-old Saramago, this was a defining image from his childhood, a defining memory. Why defining? Because it changed forever his perception of his grandfather, because it added another dimension in his experiencing and understanding of his grandfather, in his "taking in" of the world. Like Saramago, the therapist needs to capture a moment of realness from the patient's life, a metaphor, an image that reflects a real moment and adds another dimension to his understanding of the patient.

There is a growing consensus in the field that the role of the therapist is not that of the dispenser of truth, the interpreter of reality, but the facilitator, the coparticipant in a search for meaning, for aliveness. Alvarez (1992) and Ogden (1977b) both write that the therapist needs to capture the patient's psychic reality and create experiences that feel meaningful and relevant. To do that, the words and gestures used, the conveyed messages and metamessages must be alive and resonant. The therapist's task is to build a bridge between the child's world and the outer world, between the child's fear of loneliness and a persecutory absent world. Wolstein (1974) believes that psychoanalysis takes place in the area between the satisfaction of needs and the maintenance of securities, in the sharing of two people's unconscious experience, and in exploring personal meaning. Like Saramago, Ekstein (1974) talks about the need for a metaphoric language, a language that builds a bridge between conscious and preconscious, between securities and needs, where the power of the unconscious is turned from a source of endless danger to a source of creativity, a language that helps us to understand the child's mythology rather than one that seeks to translate his mythology prematurely, a language that preserves and restores the patient's creativity.

To preserve an illusion of safety, to find a common language, David was engaged in the space of his retreat, in his zone of comfort. His Internet browsing and his attempts to design his own web pages gave me a pretext to "browse" into his interests, into his sense of accomplishment and mastery. In the solitary space that was created by these activities, in the isolation of his room, he was able to experience himself as alive, to "go on being," and to preserve a sense of competence. His nocturnal emails around the world were not just escapes but also the place where he felt alive and present, the place that confirmed his yearning for contact and belonging. These activities became our "resting" places, the places to meet and chat without him feeling persecuted and pathologized. He liked my interest in his talents and seemed amused, and maybe relieved, by my obvious illiteracy with computers, with his electronic world. In retrospect, this created a symmetrical experience, a situation in which I was as ignorant and lost in his objectified world of incomprehensible speed and bewildering allure as he felt in the object world, a world full of conflicting emotions and confusing relations. His attempt to communicate and establish contact with his email messages was the bridge, the opportunity I had to find him without frightening him further away.

David spoke in short, telegraphic sentences that came out in spurts. He offered few details, mainly places, the gender of his email friends, and their interests: a Brazilian girl, a drummer from New Zealand, another musician from Stockholm, a rapper from Ireland. Minimalistic language, broad strokes, abstract images, all reflecting how distant these objects were from his life, how lonely he was, and how precarious and elusive his friendships felt. Yet, the very opacity of his descriptions offered a perfect invitation to engage with him in the transitional space, a space removed from the perceived harshness of the internal and external reality. Like Squiggle lines, his halted responses were not signs of resistance as much as beginnings, opportunities to engage with him in the dreamy space where reality and meaning are contemplated, mused, but never imposed.

David's statements invited and encouraged the formation of a third area of reality, not objective or subjective (Modell 1990), not patient-based or analyst-based (Steiner 1993), but a reality that Winnicott has called "potential space" (1971c, p. 107). It is an illusionary, transitional world that is neither inner reality nor external fact, but a space in between the subjective and objective world. In that space it was easier to inquire about his electronic friends, their music and his music, the images that Brazil and New Zealand evoked in him; it was easier to question his fantasies and his views without making him feel intruded on or exposed. There was room to ask what it was like for him to communicate all over the world, and to comment on how close these people felt in his life and yet, how absent. I could offer my I-statements, my impressions, and my observations and I could invite his reactions to them. Our interaction had gradually become a shared experience, a place where David's capacity to play and to be creative was facilitated. I could now comment on how satisfying and how sad it was at the same time to know so many people from all over the world and yet to experience them as so absent the more he got to know them, particularly the Brazilian girl, I could now add, who sounded like the kind of girl whose absence filled the room, filled his life, and changed the meaning of his life.

From there on, the theme of absence and presence was revisited numerous times in each session. He brought a beautiful poem that he wrote about a girl with whom he had been in love for years, a very bright and vivacious girl from his community, whose interest he knew—had always known—that he had no chance of attracting. It was short poem about how a simple glimpse of the girl's beauty, a "moment of beauty" as he put it, was enough to linger in him for hours, well into the "darkness of the night." Later, he brought a story and couple of weeks later a song, all about the same girl. "It's sad," I felt safe to comment, "how a girl like her fills you so much, is so present in your thoughts and yet you feel so lonely." I felt that David was making himself present in the room, was becoming more willing to make himself feel present in the room, to trust and express his yearnings and emotions, and I felt present and alive, a companion in the room. In writing a poem about that girl, in creating a poem for her, David was able to preserve her from his hate, to protect the object of his love, his imaginary companion, from becoming a persecutory reality. In writing a poem, in becoming poetic, David was able to create a "meeting place" (Winnicott 1951, p. 391), between his fantasies and his external reality, between his yearning for love and his utter loneliness.

He seemed less angry and distant as the sessions went on. He still seemed frightened and lonely, and our conversations, our relationship, still felt bumpy and at times halted, but he had made himself present, he had acknowledged my presence and there was no way back. The thoughts had become thinkable, not pretty or beautiful but thinkable, and that was an irrevocable change. He now could express his thoughts and emotions, however episodically, and he was able to observe himself and to contemplate his life. He took steps to apply to a better, more prestigious, and demanding school, and over the summer he enrolled in a preparatory program in an effort to catch up. He was still a defensive and rather distrustful youngster, but he had become more aware—less frightened—of himself, and was willing to be engaged in life, to be present, to act.

Concluding Remarks

Winnicott (1963a) conceptualizes the fear of breakdown as "a fear of a past event that has not yet been experienced" (p. 95). In their retreat, Lena and David were both avoiding processing and experiencing the past events in their lives. To avoid the processing of her mother's death, to avoid the "black hole" (Tustin 1972) in her existence and to preserve a kernel of balance, Lena had retreated into a frozen state, a state devoid of emotions and thoughts. In his bitter isolation, David insulated himself against the experience of his parents' loss and against his own overwhelming depressive anxieties. To paraphrase Winnicott (1963b), Lena's emptiness was needed in order not to feel filled up with her loss. David's anger and defiant withdrawal were also needed and served to protect him from being filled up by his own destructiveness. For both, their subjective reality and their sense of their "inside" (Tustin 1990) were so feared and so shadowed by their experience of the outside world, that reality became distorted, and understanding and processing could not be achieved and had to be forfeited. Their world was so overwhelming and persecutory that they were left with no space, no room to experience and understand (Khan 1969).

Winnicott (1971b) provides a nice example of how the experience of facilitating play, of encouraging a 2½-year-old boy with a history of emotional collapses and tantrums to discover and create in Winnicott's mirroring presence, was therapeutic for the little boy and his mother. Similarly, the experience of being allowed to discover, to participate without feeling exposed or criticized, enabled David and Lena to express their reality at their own pace, on their own terms, without becoming frightened or feeling exposed. In providing me with symbolic representations of their realities, in creating this transitional form of engagement, David and Lena became present in the room and gave me an opportunity to connect with them, to become involved with them.

Winnicott (1971a) believes that it is in playing and only in playing that the child is able to be creative and to use the whole personality. He states that "it is only in being creative that the individual discovers the self" (p. 54). But it is only in play that is mutual and playful, in which the child finds himself playing and doing without feeling observed, without having his play become pathologized, that a new experience emerges. Winnicott equates feeling creative, being creative with being alive, an experience that makes the person feel that life is meaningful and worth living. It fosters a sense of self-cohesion and purposefulness, a sense of innerness (Kristeva 1991) that changes the person's approach to external life.

The therapist's goals in working with children like Lena and David are the same as those in any other therapy, with any other patient: to facilitate growth, to restore meaning, to make the child feel more alive and hopeful, to restore trust. The therapist needs to search for, locate, and preserve the child's creative utterances, the child's moments of experiencing, however faint and uncertain. Yet, to be able to participate and facilitate the creative process, the therapist needs to experience his own creativity, needs to feel alive in his work. Without becoming poetic, without allowing himself to be reached by the patient's anxiety and fragments, what is the therapist left with? Since the predominant experience that is created in the room is that of a minus K (Bion, 1962), there is a real risk that nothing personal and meaningful will be constructed. Without the support of an image, a metaphor, without allowing himself to become fluid and poetic, the emptiness and the paralysis in the room might not be tolerated. Milner (1993) believes that when words fail to communicate the person's reality, when contact is restricted or completely abrogated, the only way for a person's psychic reality to be communicated is through symbols and metaphors. The use of symbols and metaphors, the willingness to encourage and process such acts of communication, is a poetic act. In writing about art and the evolution of man, Reid (1951) commented that the first stages of any new science or philosophy, when realities have not been constructed, the first perceptions and images are poetic in nature. I believe Reid means poetic in the full sense of the word—that is, creative—and implies that every new conception is a creative act, an act that is full of faith and passion. In allowing himself to become poetic, to experience his reverie, the therapist can capture the essence of the patient's inarticulate experience without naming it. In the bits and pieces that are projected in the room with little hope for connection and meaning, in the numbness that characterizes these patients' lives, and in the trepidation with which they approach therapy, the therapist can locate the metaphor of their existence. David's poem and nocturnal electronic chats with his invisible friends gave me an opportunity to contemplate his life, to feel and see him past his aura of false superiority and contempt. Lena's drawings not only gave me a glimpse of her world, but made it possible for me to tolerate her absence in the room, the void that she projected, without feeling insignificant and annihilated.

Ogden uses the term "reverie" (1994, 1997a,b) to describe not only the therapist's thoughts and emotions about a patient after a session, as Bion implied, but also the images, thoughts, sensations, even daydreams, that the therapist experiences during the session. For Ogden, the acts of reverie are ways of communicating with the unconscious, of becoming aware of the emotions and thoughts that are stirred in the therapist in a form that the therapist can feel and see. If this process is allowed to exist, Ogden argues, it will enable the therapist to connect with other thoughts and feelings. It is a process of containing the patient's discarded self, of understanding the patient and participating in the therapy without frightening the patient. It is a way of creating a space in which a mutual experience can be acknowledged. Kristeva (1984) believes that the individual who becomes engaged in poetic writing—and by extension in a poetic process—is able to experience his status as a subject in the world. In working with frightened patients, becoming poetic, allowing oneself to feel moved by the patient, are acts of faith (Bion 1970) that enable the therapist to transcend the deadness and paralysis in the room, to become fluid and alive, more aware of his own participation in the rhythms and movement of the session.

This is nothing new. In fact, what has attracted many psychoanalysts to the "art" of psychoanalysis is the desire to feel creative, to participate in the making and unfolding of meaning. In working with children in states of withdrawal, I believe that one should be consciously looking for a moment that draws a child out of his retreat, however briefly, that makes the child feel attuned and listened to like never before. It is not simply the insight or level of participation that makes the difference. It is the experience of being understood, of having their experiences reflected back in a manner that feels less imposing, that stimulates their ability and desire to create, engage, and experience, that has a therapeutic effect.

It is an act of knowing by "becoming" (Bion 1965), of being transformed in the process, an experience that is different from understanding and clinical insight. It is a way of capturing and filtering in the patient's experience, of creating a metaphor, and of finding a voice, a voice to communicate that is not dictated by what is "right" and what is "wrong," what is developmental or clinical. More important, it is a creative act for both the patient and the therapist, a creative moment that can be experienced and owned by both of them. Winnicott (1971b) provides a wonderful example of how the therapist's creativity, a poetic gesture that was made possible by "taking in" the child's subjective state, contributed to a moment in therapy that could be shared by both the child and Winnicott, as well as by the child's mother. Turning to a 5-year-old girl who was playing alongside while he and the girl's mother were discussing the illness of the girl's younger brother and her reaction to it, he pointed to the trinkets that she was placing on the floor next to the heads of two puppets. "Oh look!," he exclaimed, "You are putting on the floor around these babies' heads the dreams that they are having while they are asleep" (p. 45).

Until such a language is created, until the therapist finds his "voice," his poetry, his metaphors, he might not be able to understand his own experiences and the patient's subjectivity, and the external world might be distorted (Winnicott 1951) or used as a substitute for understanding (Bion 1970). The thoughts will still be unthinkable and the experiences will still not be experienced.

Noticing that every good therapeutic encounter involves and stimulates the therapist's creativity and art, Winnicott (1954) wondered what patient wants to be someone else's poem or artistic creation. Yet, without becoming poetic, without feeling moved and changed by the patient's life, by the patient's attempts to express his life, to find meaning and purpose in his life, psychoanalytic psychotherapy runs the risk of becoming a technical and joyless process. The question, therefore, can be reversed; What therapist wants to only feel and experience himself as a good, even flawless, technician, and for that matter what patient wants to be someone else's technical accomplishment?

REFERENCES

Alvarez, A. (1992). *Live Company: Psychoanalytic Psychotherapy with Autistic, Borderline, Deprived and Abused Children*. London: Routledge.

Balint, M. (1968). *The Basic Fault: Therapeutic Aspects of Regression*. London: Tavistock.

Bion, W. R. (1957). Differentiation of the psychotic from the nonpsychotic personalities. In *Second Thoughts*, pp. 43–64. Northvale, NJ: Aronson, 1967.

——— (1959). A theory of thinking. In *Second Thoughts*, pp. 110–119. Northvale, NJ: Aronson, 1967.

——— (1962). *Learning from Experience*. New York: Basic Books.

——— (1963). *Elements of Psychoanalysis*. London: Heinemann; reprinted, Northvale, NJ: Aronson, 1979.

——— (1965). *Transformations*. London: Heinemann; reprinted, London: Karnac, 1984.

——— (1970). *Attention and Interpretation*. London: Heinemann; reprinted, London: Karnac, 1984.

Eigen, M. (1996). *Psychic Deadness*. Northvale, NJ: Aronson.

Ekstein, R. (1974). Towards Walden III. *Journal of Loma Linda University School of Medicine* 28(2):5–17.

——— (1983a). Play therapy for borderline children. In *Handbook of Play Therapy*, ed. C. E. Schaefer and K. J. O'Connor, pp. 412–418. New York: Wiley.

——— (1983b). *Children of Time and Space, Action and Impulse*. New York: Aronson.

Grotstein, J. (1978). Inner Space: its dimensions and its coordinates. *International Journal of Psychoanalysis*, Vol. 59, pp. 55–61.

Josephs, B. (1983). On understanding and not understanding: some technical issues. *International Journal of Psycho-Analysis* 64:291–298.

Khan, M. (1969). Vicissitudes of being, knowing and experiencing in the therapeutic situation. In *The Privacy of the Self.* Madison, CT: International Universities Press, 1974.

Kristeva, J. (1984). *Revolution in Poetic Language*, trans. M. Waller. New York: Columbia University Press.

——— (1991). *Strangers to Ourselves*, trans. L. Roudiez. New York: Columbia University Press.

McDougall, J. (1984). The disaffected patient: reflections on affect and pathology. *Psychoanalytic Quarterly* 53(2):386–409.

Meltzer, D. (1975). *Explorations in Autism: A Psycho-Analytical Study*. Perthshire, Scotland: Clunie.

Milner, M. (1993). The role of illusion in symbol formation. In *Transitional*

Objects and Potential Spaces: Literary Uses of D. W. Winnicott, ed. P. L. Rudnytsky, pp. 13–39. New York: Columbia University Press.

Modell, A. H. (1990). The roots of creativity and the use of the object. In *Tactics and Techniques in Psychoanalytic Therapy: III The Implications of Winnicott's Contributions,* ed. P. L. Giovacchini, pp. 113–127. Northvale, NJ: Aronson.

Newirth, J. (1996). On not interpreting: the metaphor of the baby, enactment and transitional experience. *The American Journal of Psychoanalysis* 56(4):415–429.

Ogden, T. H. (1986). *The Matrix of the Mind.* Northvale, NJ: Aronson.

——— (1989). *The Primitive Edge of Experience.* Northvale, NJ: Aronson.

——— (1994). The analytic third—working with intersubjective clinical facts. *International Journal of Psycho-Analysis* 75:3–20.

——— (1997a). Reverie and metaphor: some thoughts on how I work as a psychoanalyst. *International Journal of Psycho-Analysis* 78:719–732.

——— (1997b). *Reverie and Interpretation: Sensing Something Human.* Northvale, NJ: Aronson.

Reid, H. (1951). *Art and the Evolution of Man.* London: Freedom.

Slade, A. (1994). *Making Meaning and Making Believe: Their Role in the Clinical Process*, ed. A. Slade and D. Palmer Wolf, pp. 81–107. New York: Oxford University Press.

Steiner, J. (1993). *Psychic Retreats: Pathological Organizations in Psychotic, Neurotic and Borderline Patients.* London: Routledge.

Stolorow, R., and Atwood, G. (1992). *Context of Being: The Intersubjective Foundation of Psychological Life.* Hillside, NJ: Analytic Press.

Tustin, F. (1972). *Autism and Childhood Psychosis.* London: Hogarth.

——— (1980). Autistic objects. *International Review of Psycho-Analysis* 61:27–40.

——— (1984). Autistic shapes. *International Review of Psychoanalysis* 65:279–290.

——— (1986). *Autistic Barriers in Neurotic Patients.* New Haven, CT: Yale University Press.

——— (1990). *The Protective Shell in Children and Adults.* London: Karnac.

Winnicott, D. W. (1951). Marion Milner: Critical Notice on Not Being Able to Paint, ed. C. Winnicott, R. Shepherd, and M. Davis, pp. 390–392. Cambridge, MA: Harvard University Press.

——— (1954). Metapsychological and clinical aspects of regression within the psycho-analytical setup. In *Collected Papers / D. W. Winnicott*, ed. C. Winnicott, R. Shepherd, and M. Davis, pp. 278–294. Cambridge, MA: Harvard University Press, 1989.

——— (1963a). Fear of breakdown. In *Psycho-Analytic Explorations*, ed. C. Winnicott, R. Shepherd, and M. Davis, pp. 87–95. Cambridge, MA: Harvard University Press.

——— (1963b). Communicating and not communicating leading to a study of certain opposites. In *The Maturational Processes and the Facilitating Environment*, pp. 179–192. New York: International Universities Press, 1965.

——— (1971a). Playing: creative activity and the search for the self. *Playing and Reality*. pp. 53–64. New York: Basic Books.

——— (1971b). Playing: a theoretical statement. In *Playing and Reality*, pp. 38–52. New York: Basic Books.

——— (1971c). The place where we live. In *Playing and Reality*, pp. 104–110. New York: Basic Books.

Wolstein, B. (1974). Individuality and identity. *Contemporary Psychoanalysis* 14(1):1–14.

JicaP Vol. 2, No. 2, 2002

Introduction

Elizabeth Kandall, Ph.D.

The following paper and discussion were presented at the second Spring Meeting of the Children's Psychotherapy Project, NY on April 19, 2001 at the William Alanson White Institute. This was the first time a treatment from the Project was presented to the larger community and as such it marked a milestone in our development.

The Children's Psychotherapy Project is a simply structured social action project for therapists. Therapists who join the Project are asked to take on one foster child in a once weekly psychotherapy, providing collateral contacts as needed "for as long as it takes." Weekly consultation groups are run by a senior clinician. We believe that these groups are necessary and an integral part of any long-term therapy with this population. Our entirely volunteer organization is inspired by and modeled after the Children's Psychotherapy Project in San Francisco, which has been going strong for eight years now. There they see forty children and have ten consultation groups. The Project in New York started with a core group of founding members: Christopher Bonovitz, Psy.D., Neil Altman, Ph.D., Kate Dunn, Psy.D., and Elizabeth Kandall, Ph.D., who met weekly for a year to discuss and plan for the Project in New York. The Children's Psychotherapy Project, NY started seeing children in February of 2001. At the time of this writing thirteen children are in treatment and we have five consultation groups. We have gotten the bulk of our referrals from the Administration of Children's Services direct care but have also made contacts with Legal Aid both in Manhattan and Brooklyn, as well as private foster care agencies. We are open to working with other referral sources and to welcoming more therapists into the Project. To learn more about the Children's Psychotherapy Project contact Toni Heineman at (415) 474-8454 or tvh@itsa.ucsf.edu or Elizabeth Kandall at (212) 255–8895 or ejkandall@aol.com.

THE PRESENTERS

Neil Altman is a Founding Member of the Children's Psychotherapy Project in New York. He both leads a consultation group and sees an adolescent through the Project. Neil's work has done much to bring together social issues and psychoanalytic thought. He bravely approaches topics such as poverty, racism, politics, bureaucracy, and all the personal, uncomfortable feelings they bring in order to offer a truly dialectic approach to individual and social issues. He has done this through scholarly understanding of complex social and psychic factors, often weaving together an enlightening perspective not even approached by others. But he has done this most, I think, through a deep personal refusal to be sideswiped by pretension and social convention. He has moved far beyond received knowledge about what we analyze and what we leave outside the consulting room to bring a fresh and original vision to psychoanalysis. He has shown us how facing the difficult and dark aspects of society is as important as facing the difficult and dark aspects of ourselves, and that the two are not actually so different. His legacy of bridging public and private sectors both psychically and socially is central to the spirit of the Children's Psychotherapy Project.

For nearly eight years Toni Heineman has been involved in the development and direction of the Children's Psychotherapy Project in California. The project has been, in her words, "saving the lives of children who otherwise would have no reliable external object or sustainable connection to their internal worlds." Toni describes the idea for the Project coming to her one day when she got a call from someone needing a low-fee therapist. She had no time available. So she called around to see who else might have a spot, but everyone's calendar was full. She realized we needed to build a longer list of available people. She tells this story with such ordinariness and ease that only later did I realize how utopian a vision it was. There was a confidence and an assumption that there are enough people to help, and that a few phone calls should be able to do it. Working around her one can feel the contagious optimism. I have begun to see how this can happen.

JicaP Vol. 2, No. 2, 2002

Geraldine: On the Way Out of Foster Care

Neil Altman, Ph.D.

Eighteen-year-old Geraldine looked me directly in the eye: "My mother shouldn't have had children." I looked back at her, unblinking, stunned. She wasn't saying she wished she hadn't been born. She was making a clear observation about her mother who discovered, after she had Geraldine, that she liked the idea of children much better than the reality. Geraldine had been explaining to me why her mother had been so violent with her when they had lived together, why she had slammed her face down on the table so hard, when she was 9 years old, that her nose was broken. Geraldine's father had come home, seen the blood and the deformed nose, and had beaten up Geraldine's mother. Afterwards, Geraldine's mother had been terribly remorseful, tearful. She didn't hate Geraldine most of the time, but there was no one else to blame for the premature loss of her freedom, her youth, when she was 19 years old. Actually, the "father" who beat up Geraldine's mother turned out to be a stepfather. Geraldine had always wondered why no one else in the family had her last name. It was not until she was 14 that she learned, from a cousin, that her father was someone else. This cousin offered to introduce her to her father's family, and eventually she met her biological father.

Two years later, there was another daughter, after Geraldine's mother married the man Geraldine thought was her father. By the time this daughter, Lourdes, was born, Geraldine's mother was so heavily into drugs that an aunt took over Lourdes's care soon after she was born. When Lourdes was still an infant, Geraldine's mother was convicted on a drug charge and spent some time in jail. Geraldine was placed in kinship foster care, the first of a number of placements with her maternal grandparents. Lourdes lives with the aunt and her husband to this day. A son and two more daughters were later born to Geraldine's mother and stepfather. They all live with their maternal grandparents at this time, since both their mother and father are in jail, the mother on an immigration charge, the father probably on a drug charge. Geraldine takes her youngest three siblings to see their mother in jail every week. She hopes her mother gets out of jail soon to prevent the adoption of Lourdes by her aunt.

Geraldine now lives in a group home. She was living with her maternal grandparents until recently. An aunt, who lives with the grandparents, had resented Geraldine since Geraldine had displaced her as the youngest child in the family some fifteen years ago when Geraldine was first placed in kinship foster care. Geraldine thought her aunt set her up to look bad to the grandparents, in the latest incident, by taking a call from Geraldine saying that she was going to stay overnight at a friend's house, then not telling the grandparents so that they would think that Geraldine was out all night without checking in. On this last occasion Geraldine had attacked her aunt physically, bloodying her face. This incident led to Geraldine's being placed in the group home. Geraldine has some history of physical violence. She spent a month in a juvenile detention center when she was 16, when the mother of a girl she hit pressed charges. There have been several occasions on which Geraldine has hit people, men and women, when she felt they were treating her disrespectfully. Geraldine has a long-term boyfriend with whom she is sexually active; she is a scrupulous user of birth control (she is intent on not following in her mother's footsteps, although she has had one abortion). Geraldine worked until recently as a cashier, but she was fired for cursing out her boss when he accused her of mishandling some money. She faithfully attends her GED classes daily, planning to get her own apartment as soon as possible, and probably go to college. There is, in the history I was given, a report that she was raped in her early teen years. I have not heard about this from Geraldine.

I have seen Geraldine once weekly since early February. She is moderately overweight, of Latina background; her mother is from South America, her biological and stepfathers from the Caribbean. I will now present a session from late March.

As Geraldine settled into her chair, having arrived five minutes early by group home-arranged taxi, I asked her how she was. Her face looked unsettled: "I was fired." "Oh." I, too, felt unsettled, a bit guilty, having heard the previous week about her conflicts with her boss at work. She had described how he talked to her in a high-handed and disrespectful manner and how she responded to him in kind. I tried to remember whether I had asked her if she thought she might get fired, trying to assuage my guilt associated with feeling that I had failed to warn her about this outcome, inevitable in retrospect. I remembered that she had said that she would never talk disrespectfully to the *big* boss who she knew would summarily dismiss her. Her boyfriend got fired this week too. They're supposed to get a day off each week, but the boss asked him to work every day. So he just didn't show up on Friday. Saturday, Geraldine had been hoping to have the day off because it was her sister's birthday, but was told to come to work at 9 A.M. She showed up at 10, hoping to be sent home, but the boss didn't say anything. At the end of the day, however, she had misplaced a credit card receipt, her boss accused her of incompetence, and she had a flash of rage: let him try to find someone else who is as careful as she is with paper work. She also had ten dollars too *much* in her register. He rolled his eyes. "What the fuck is wrong with you??? I'm giving you too *much* money!!! I could've put that ten dollars in my pocket!!!" "You curse at me one more time and you're fired." "FUCK YOU!!!"

"Maybe I was wrong, but he was too." I asked Geraldine if, in retrospect, she thought she could have avoided being fired by swallowing her pride at that moment and not responding to his provocation. She said it was all she could do *only* to curse at him then. She had really wanted to punch him out.

O—K— I thought. Let me readjust my expectations. "I *did* hit someone this week," Geraldine went on. "You know how crowded it is on the 7 train? I told my friend we shouldn't take the 7 train, I was too upset, people pushing and shoving, I was going to get set off. She said, 'Come on, you'll be OK.' So I'm standing on the platform and this guy is bothering us. 'Where you going, girls?' 'None of your business' 'Ooooh, tough girls, huh?' 'Get out of my face—!' The train pulled in and we got on. We're all crowded together and he standing right in front of me and he puts his arm around me. I pushed his arm off me and he patted my head. At the station when he got off, my friend and I got off too. She held him and I punched him. You should've seen the look in his eyes. He never thought a girl would hit him. We got back into the train before the doors closed."

"You're lucky there was no cop on the platform. You could've been arrested and you don't want a record."

"Oh, I've already been arrested. But now that I'm 18 my juvenile record is expunged. Good thing. No, I don't want an adult record."

"How did you get arrested?"

"One time my friends and I were arrested for trespassing. There was an abandoned building across the street from the East New York group home. Me and my friends used to sit on the stoop and smoke. One day these plain clothes cops come by and said, 'Why don't you girls go home?' 'We *are* home!' 'Move off the steps and go home!' We just sat there and they took us in for trespassing on city property. I've been in a lot of fights. One time the mother of the girl I hit pressed charges and I ended up staying in the Juvenile Detention facility in the Bronx for a month."

"Spofford?!"

"Yes."

"That must've been awful."

"It was."

"So when your boss said he'd fire you if you cursed one more time you had such a flash of anger, a physical thing, you were trying not to hit him."

"Yes—. I'm just like my mother. And my father. There was a lot of hitting in my family. One time my mother broke my nose."

"How?"

"Smashing my head down on the table."

I stare at her wide-eyed. She's twisting her nose around to show how it's still bent.

"How old were you?"

"Nine. There was all this blood and my nose was bent out of shape. See—it still is. When my father got home and he saw my nose, he beat up my mother."

"Did she feel bad later, or—?"

"Terrible. She cried and said she was sorry. She couldn't control herself—. My mother shouldn't have had children—. She needed her freedom. She was only 19 when I was born."

"Just a year older than you are now. No wonder you're so determined not to have a child for a while."

"You got it. She liked the *idea* of children, but not having to take care of them. I understand. I want to go to college and I want to party for a couple of years—. Oh, I just remembered, I'm supposed to get a letter from you *every* time I come here to prove I actually came—. Sorry."

"That's no problem. I should see if the car service called—."

"You'd think the taxi voucher would be enough—."

"Good point!! Sometimes you just have to go along with bureaucracies—."

In concluding, I want to raise the question of the impact of the structure of the project on patients and therapists. No money is involved in the Children's Psychotherapy Project and the therapist's commitment is to see the child once a week for as long as is needed. Geraldine had been in therapy once before, at a clinic, with a therapist who turned out to be a student. In our first session, Geraldine told me, with anger, that in her fourth session, she was told by the therapist that she was finishing her placement and that would be their last session. At that point, feeling quite virtuous, I said that the point of this project was that therapists like me were *volunteering* time in our private offices to see foster children *for as long as they needed to be seen.* I wonder now about my investment in avoiding a "bad object" transference, setting myself up as "good," unlike bad therapists and parents who abandon their charges. Along related lines, I wonder about my alliance with Geraldine against "bad" authority figures like her boss, and the authorities in her group home who require a letter from me documenting her attendance at every session, as evidenced by my saying "good point" when she noted that a taxi voucher served the same function. On one hand, I share her annoyance; on the other I do not want to collude with keeping the badness "out there," which might perpetuate a pattern of run-ins with authority figures in the world, while I sympathize with how unfair the world is. This seems to me a dilemma partially inherent in the set-up of the Children's Psychotherapy Project, which does encourage us to feel like "good" objects in the lives of these children who have had enough "bad" object experiences already.

JicaP Vol. 2, No. 2, 2002

Not for Love or Money: A Discussion of a Case Presentation by Neil Altman

Toni Vaughn Heineman, D.M.H.

Before turning to Dr. Altman's thought-provoking presentation of his work with Geraldine, I'd like to address some of the issues he raises at the end of his remarks. Obviously, questions of financial and emotional gratification are inherent in the structure of any therapeutic relationship. Certainly we are also aware of the complex interplay of perpetrator/victim that informs the transference–countertransference paradigms in our treatment of children who have been neglected or abused. However, Dr. Altman suggests that the particular structure of The Children's Psychotherapy Project may bring some of these questions into sharper than usual relief, and I think we can productively use this opportunity to consider them.

While I was preparing this talk, three vignettes about payment for psychotherapy came to mind that I'd like to share with you.

First, a tale from many years ago when I was a teaching assistant for Judy Wallerstein, who had recently moved to the Bay Area from Topeka: She sometimes talked about a gentleman who "visited" with Karl Menninger on a weekly basis. They often chatted about the weather, a very important topic in the farming communities of Kansas. Sometimes they discussed the current prices of wheat or hog backs; sometimes the conversations turned to more personal topics. At the end of each meeting this gentleman handed Dr. Menninger a dozen eggs that he had carefully gathered from his hen house.

Moving to the present: I have been working with a little girl, now aged 7, for a bit over two years. Her parents bring her regularly and pay my full fee promptly each month. I find her absolutely charming—much of the time. At other times I am subjected to the obstinate whining and stubborn refusals with which she tortures her mother on a daily basis. Generally we work well and hard together. In other words, this is an ideal case, except for one problem—she isn't improving as much or as quickly as either her mother or I think she should. I mention this example in today's context because for about the last eighteen months I have rather been expecting her parents to "fire" me. Why shouldn't they—they're paying very good money for not very good results.

Now, stepping back in time a bit to one of the first gatherings of the full membership of the Children's Psychotherapy Project in San Francisco and a discussion of money and the feelings about working for no pay if there was actually money available to pay for treatment for some of these children. Early in the conversation, one of the most junior therapists timidly offered that she felt a particular sense of pleasure at the end of the month when, faced with a pile of unwritten statements and forms demanding completion, she arrived at the name of the child she was seeing through the Project. There was no paperwork!

The discussion continued about the feelings attendant on giving freely and the sense of working without the monthly reminder of "The Department" standing between therapist and child. Talking about the consequences of the resentment that can and does build from feeling overworked, underpaid, and undervalued aroused a more heated discussion. In San Francisco the rate of $55/hour for psychotherapy with foster children and parents, which prevailed six years ago, remains unchanged today, while private practice fees have kept pace with the (until recently) booming economy.

One of our purposes in structuring the Project the way we did was to develop a program that was truly based on "fee for service," rather than the prevailing "fee for degree." Along with providing services to children, we embarked on this Project with a sense of adventure and a feeling that we (psychologists, social workers, psychiatrists, analysts, and family counselors) were all in this together. The fee for service is the same, that is, "nothing." The most junior therapists and the most senior consultants receive identical financial compensation for their contributions to the Project. This structure does not pretend that there are no differences among us in skill, experience, vitality, or hopefulness; it does announce that in this Project we have joined forces for a mutually valued undertaking, to which we will all make unique contributions and from which we will each reap different benefits.

Doesn't this sound like a nice and cozy arrangement? Collaboration, cooperation, sharing, and mutually satisfying clinical education and edification. What happened to aggression, competition, and (even) one-upmanship? As Dr. Altman notes, working without payment can certainly establish and maintain our sense of being one of the few good objects in the lives of these children and adolescents whose worlds are often so filled with bad objects. However, we know that there are no internal or external worlds without bad objects. If, by virtue of our altruism, we banish the bad guys from our organization, where do we and our young patients find them?

Through our discussions in the consultation groups that actually sustain the work of the Project, we've discovered that if we aren't careful we can conveniently contain most of the bad guys within "the system." The rules and regulations are often absurd, the biological parents repeatedly don't make it to their promised visits, the foster parents are frequently insensitive to the children in their care, the social workers are notoriously unresponsive and incompetent, the children's attorneys don't have time to work their caseloads diligently, and the judges attend to the law rather than to the children. There is no shortage of neglectful, abusive, or simply unfair reality to fuel the anger we carry on behalf of our young patients.

I think Dr. Altman is correct in noting that, in these situations, we are more tempted than usual to identify with our patients' relatively unambivalent world-views. Because we recognize the enormity of our vicarious rage we are eager to close the consulting room door against the evils and hurts of the world; both consciously and unconsciously we often long to create a haven of safety and innocence for our young patients.

Keep the vignettes in mind while we turn to Geraldine: About two months into therapy, safely past the dangers of abandonment she associates with the fourth session, she begins to tell us her true story of good guys and bad guys. There are unfair bosses, predators who ride the subways, cops who seemingly have nothing better to do than harass young girls. There are even parents who hit each other and their children, sometimes breaking bones.

However, these pale in comparison to the dangers of a child who carries within her the power to destroy a mother's life. In this very brief interchange Geraldine introduces us to the destructive forces that she experiences within herself. She explains that her mother needed her freedom. She doesn't blame her mother; she understands. Geraldine announces that she does not intend to let a child ruin *her* future in the way that she ripped away her mother's chances for a full and pleasurable life—a life that might have included time for learning from adults and playing with friends. Dr. Altman's comment, "No wonder you're so determined not to have a child for a while," acknowledges Geraldine's belief that children can and do kill parents—in spirit, if not in fact. Momentarily, Geraldine and Dr. Altman are joined in a shared recognition that, while the door may be closed against some bad guys, a sense of evil and destructive forces must be part of their relationship. The real and true villain is in the room and they are confronting her.

This announcement of the deadly aspects of herself are too much to bear for more than a moment. Geraldine suddenly remembers that she needs "proof of attendance," not just from the taxi driver, but a personal letter from her therapist. With this, she opens the door to the ostracized bad guys. Not surprisingly, Dr. Altman, undoubtedly with more than a little relief, accepts Geraldine's offer to side with her against them and invites them in. Who wouldn't? After all, following up on her earlier warning that she drives therapists away, Geraldine has just issued a more forceful admonition, albeit tangentially, that she is a patient with enormous and frightening powers. The group home's requirement of a letter from her therapist allows her the opportunity to ask not only whether Dr. Altman will be there for every session, but whether they will survive their sessions together. Will he have sufficient strength to contain her feelings and enough caring to send the required reassurances to the outside world? Will she emerge physically and psychologically intact, able to show proof of a relationship that can withstand her inherent badness?

In this session Geraldine and Dr. Altman illustrate the beginnings of a very serious undertaking. Sorting through the complexities of Geraldine's feelings, impulses, thoughts, fantasies, desires, and relationships will not be easy. I think we can safely venture a guess that her wishes to have a life different from and better than her mother's will not come to fruition without considerable and sustained effort. Although at this point we don't know very much about Geraldine's inner life, we can reasonably suppose that her worries about killing or damaging others contribute, at least in part, to her actually risking being hurt or killed by others. She is engaged in a life-and-death struggle, which will inevitably and inexorably play itself out if they can engage in a successful therapeutic relationship.

In his parting comment, suggesting that sometimes we are better served by "playing along," Dr. Altman introduces the wonderful freedom of play into the relationship. He suggests that together they can behave "as if" proof of attendance somehow legitimizes their work together. This is not colluding with an unconscious fantasy; it is a conscious and deliberate articulation of their shared, humorous view of one of life's absurdities.

Dr. Altman correctly notes that a very great danger in working with Geraldine lies in the pull to collude with her unconscious projection of her own intolerable sense of badness into authority figures, whom she hates and demeans because they cannot protect her or others from her destructiveness. However, if patient and therapist can play cops and robbers, or good guys and bad guys, that is, if they can build a relationship that can contain both good and bad, and can allow for each of them to hold and play both roles without anyone's truly getting hurt, then Geraldine has a chance of escaping the real life-and-death struggle that now controls her existence. While her relationship with Dr. Altman may save Geraldine's life, it will also, like any other therapeutic endeavor, exact an emotional, if not a financial, price.

And what will be Dr. Altman's return on his investment? Not money in the bank. This treatment isn't going to pay the mortgage or fund the retirement account. Not love. The questions he raises point to a shared code of personal and professional ethics that does not allow us to demand emotional payment from our patients as a substitute for financial remuneration. How then do we guard against becoming entrapped in the notion that a life saved is a life owed?

Perhaps Karl Menninger and his patient can offer us the beginning of an answer. It seems that somehow these two gentlemen agreed that one dozen eggs was proper payment for one hour of psychotherapy. Clearly, half a dozen was not enough and two dozen was too much, a reminder that fair is what people agree is fair.

Perhaps as Geraldine moves more into adulthood she will feel that being seen for free isn't fair, but that she really can't afford to pay more than the price of a dozen eggs. In a similar situation in San Francisco, a young woman who was being seen through the Project began working, and therefore wanted to begin paying for her therapy. The fee she could afford was so low that it didn't feel fair to either patient or therapist. She suggested that she would like to make regular donations to the Children's Psychotherapy Project. They continued their work together, each contributing to a mutually valued program. This illustrates a way in which a discussion about fees can provide a forum for considering the value of the therapeutic relationship.

I would suggest that fees (or their lack) do not significantly differ from all of the other realities that define and impinge upon a therapeutic relationship, in that each provides a forum for discussion and negotiation of the relationship's central conflicts and the psychic energy that drives it. For example, a little boy with intense sibling rivalry may experience my every absence or schedule change as a displacement to make room for a more desirable patient, while a young woman with a pathologically inattentive mother may interpret breaks and schedule changes as evidence that I simply cannot keep her schedule or needs in my mind. Patients who live in constant fear of abandonment may panic at the thought of delaying a payment for a week or so, even if they have a legitimate reason, while others delay payment for the anxiety-driven pleasure of withholding, rather than waiting for, gratification.

My worry about getting "fired" by the mother of my "almost ideal" little patient provides a different example of an externalization of a central psychic issue in a therapeutic relationship. My concern about the quality of my work paralleled this family's pervasive intergenerational anxiety about the adequacy of parenting. My fears of being fired reflected my consciously held knowledge that this family shopped well and carefully, expecting to get what they paid for. More slowly, I came to understand how the severe disappointments passed from parents to children in this family had set the stage for their quickly discarding potentially inadequate relationships. These "firings" attempted to avert the intolerable despondency that would surely follow the expected emotional neglect and abandonment. Even more slowly, I came to recognize this family's quiet longing for a good enough relationship that bound them to me. I believe they stayed with me because I could hold for and with them the possibilities of my own inadequacies, which were more than usually stirred by their expectations of failure and disappointment. Like Geraldine, I felt that what I gave just wouldn't be enough. However, unlike Geraldine, I could contain and try to understand the feelings rather than needing to force a "firing" in order to be rid of them.

Dr. Altman reminds us that working "for free" may leave us vulnerable to a rigid definition of ourselves as the "good guys," sent to rescue these children from the "bad guys" who permeate their internal and external worlds. For our work to be successful, we must move beyond pathologically generated stereotypes of ourselves or our patients. Any unarticulated and unanalyzed feelings about the realities that we and our patients necessarily impose on our work—such as fees, schedules and schedule changes, or interruptions for holidays—can leave us vulnerable to all sorts of internal and interpersonal distortions of self and other within the therapeutic relationship. This work is hard to do alone. We turn to colleagues, supervisors, and consultants for help in understanding the ways in which our feelings are impeding or promoting our therapeutic work.

I must observe to you, by way of conclusion, that some six or seven years into the Children's Psychotherapy Project in San Francisco, we do not feel that we are working for free. Perhaps some of those who have dropped by the wayside have felt underpaid. In my experience, we who remain feel quite richly compensated by our participation in the Project. My meeting with the members of my consultation group constitutes one of the highlights of my week. Over bag lunches we debrief, discuss the most recent frustrations with "the system," attempt to understand thoughts and feelings about therapeutic impasses and breakthroughs, commiserate over the frequent tedium of the work, consider the particular ways in which an article we've read together pertains to work with foster children, and usually leave feeling refreshed by the company and revived by the intellectual stimulation.

Of course, like analytic or therapeutic sessions, some of these discussions are more satisfying than others. However, in a process that parallels therapy or analysis, a coherent whole gradually develops out of these weekly meetings. They both bind the members of each consultation group and join the various groups through shared readings and periodic larger meetings. Most important, our contacts with these patients, their parents, foster parents, teachers, and social workers continually remind us of their need for sustained and sustaining relationships. Likewise, in our consultation groups, meetings with invited speakers, and casual contacts with fellow Project members at parties, in neighborhood coffee shops, or at professional meetings, we are reminded of our own need for sustained and sustaining relationships. We have created a community of which we are proud and which holds us warmly in its embrace. I invite you to join us. It presents an opportunity not to be missed.

(To learn more about The Children's Psychotherapy Project and the possibility of establishing a chapter in your community, you may contact Dr. Heineman at (415) 474-8454 or 2481 Clay St. #201, San Francisco, CA 94115.)

JicaP Vol. 2, No. 2, 2002

Beyond Love and Money: Response to Discussion

Neil Altman, Ph.D.

Dr. Heineman's discussion was one of the most illuminating commentaries on my work I have ever encountered. Most important, she answered my question about the location of the "bad" object in my work with Geraldine simply and clearly, by noting how Geraldine was revealing a sense of overwhelming destructiveness in her narrative of her personal history. This narrative, her life itself, was founded on the idea that she had destroyed her mother's life by being born. Once one recognizes this feeling of destructiveness, a core issue in the therapy is framed: Will Geraldine and I survive her destructiveness, thus providing a chance of reworking this core aspect of her being? In this connection, the question about me, representing her internal object, has to do with my strength, my survivability.

I regret to say that Geraldine stopped coming to sessions shortly after this case presentation. I would now interpret her termination of our work as reflecting unmanageable anxiety that we would not be able to survive her destructiveness, to contain it within our relationship. Perhaps my failure to recognize her sense of destructiveness in our early sessions itself was interpreted by Geraldine as evidence that I lacked the ability to contain, to survive her destructive impact. I look back and imagine myself sitting in the room with her, listening to her account of her own beginnings, recognizing the feeling that her very existence had so disrupted her mother's life. The despair attendant to this recognition would indeed have been hard to bear. It would have been even more difficult to say something to Geraldine that contained this horrible recognition. Geraldine camouflaged her sense of destructiveness, hiding it from both me and from herself, in a discussion of why she was so determined not to have a child at too young an age. I was focused on Geraldine's wish not to repeat her mother's mistakes. If my reverie, at the time, had been more free to float, I would surely have lit upon the implications for Geraldine's sense of self of this foundational story.

One sees here the workings of anxiety, the way in which difficult-to-bear experiences, quickly recognized when pointed out by another who is looking at the situation more dispassionately, can be excluded from awareness. Geraldine's later account of violence on the subway platform can be seen as a further unconscious effort on her part to bring her destructiveness to the table.

With respect to money, I wonder whether the fact that I was not being paid further added to Geraldine's anxiety about my survivability. If money compensates therapists for the psychic work entailed in suffering with their patients, the absence of such compensation might make a patient question, unconsciously, whether a therapist would be willing to be exposed to such feelings. The absence of monetary compensation might also affect patients' unconscious sense of entitlement to put their therapists through such experiences.

One reason, among many others, that I value Dr. Heineman's vision of the Children's Psychotherapy Project is that it allows us to imagine and to play out, to some degree, what it would be like to be therapists and patients if money were not an issue. It is very difficult in our society, as Heineman intimates, to escape from the pervasive significance of money as virtually synonymous with value. As I indicated just above, the absence of money can have as much meaning in terms of money-as-value as a very high fee. Even in our capitalistic society, however, we do have a concept of "pricelessness," and Heineman has established a structure to make possible priceless experiences. There are, indeed, times when I come to resent having compromised on my fee with a patient who makes me suffer. But it is part of the priceless value of psychotherapy, as I conceive of the process, that grappling with suffering in therapy always has the potential for yielding personal growth for therapist and patient alike. I am grateful to Toni Heineman for imagining, and putting into practice, a structure that facilitates *free* therapy, in the sense of a degree of freedom from the constraints of money.

Afterword: Response to Neil Altman

Toni Vaughn Heineman, D.M.H.

I think Dr. Altman's thoughtful and very generous response to my comments is a very good parallel to what happens in the Project's consultation groups. For a variety of reasons and in a variety of ways we are sometimes prevented from thinking about the exceedingly difficult issues that confront us when we sit in a therapy session with these young people. I don't think it's true that Dr. Altman doesn't have an "internal map" for "locating the bad object," only that something in the relationship with Geraldine made it temporarily unavailable to him. One of the functions of the consultation groups is to provide a collective memory—we can hold outside the hour what can/must be temporarily forgotten in the hour.

This reminds me of a situation in my consultation group in which a therapist became extremely distressed about the behavior of her adolescent patient. She felt that he was becoming so belligerent, irresponsible, rude, and just generally morally reprehensible in all of his relationships that she should call a meeting of all of the (many) adults in his life to try to understand and correct this problem. After listening to her worry about this young man, toward whom she usually responded with empathy and affection, the group members reminded her that both of his parents had died violent deaths in the previous two months. The therapist obviously "knew" this, but the knowledge was too much for her to bear. Her idea of gathering a cadre of protective adults expressed many wishes, including her wanting to demonstrate that "all was not lost" and that she was not alone with this child's grief. The group's capacity to hold this terrible reality for and with her supplied the necessary support to free her to attend to the needs of her patient. These comments merely echo Dr. Altman's sense that with free therapy may come the freedom to think and play which must include thinking about freedom and its inherent constraints.

JicaP Vol. 2, No. 2, 2002

Interactive Movement Patterns as Ports of Entry in Infant–Parent Psychotherapy: Ways of Seeing Nonverbal Behavior

K. Mark Sossin, Ph.D.

When observing and describing an infant's shifting level of arousal, facial gesture, or kicking rhythm, or when appraising face-to-face social interaction, parental sensitivity, or any of the myriad other behaviors we deem developmentally and clinically relevant, what fashions the lens through which the infant–parent psychotherapist makes observations? What determines the descriptive language used? How do this lens and language influence the attributions made by the clinician?

The subject of this paper[1] is the nature of our data: we are closely observing infants and parents and drawing clinical conclusions, but we are doing so without a shared lexicon for the nonverbal behaviors observed. Do some nonverbal behaviors have predetermined meaning? Are there dimensions and patterns of nonverbal behavior that have intrinsic links to levels of psychic functioning and individual psychological proclivities, and if so, what units of behavior are meaningful? In highlighting the value of systematic and coherent approaches to nonverbal behavior, the ways in which behaviors are often observed and identified are examined. Careful observational research has prompted significant advances in theory pertaining to the mutually influencing parent–infant intrapsychic representations of the social world (Beebe and Lachmann 1998, Fonagy 1994, Tronick 1998). Yet it seems possible that insufficient attention has been paid to the selective nature of the behaviors observed and catalogued (as well as those that are not).

The task of identifying which nonverbal patterns are pertinent for the infant–parent psychotherapist, or even defining what establishes a mean-

1. The author wishes to thank Katrina Adams, doctoral student in psychology at Pace University for contributing her comments regarding infant observation methods, and Drs. Jan Charone-Sossin and Anni Bergman for their critical reading of this manuscript.

ingfully distinguished nonverbal pattern at all, has often followed from intuition or a sense of face-validity. In this paper, the importance of seeing patterns relevant to the tasks of the infant–parent psychotherapist is reviewed. The theoretical and research anchors for these classification schemes are described, especially in light of the formalized systems, evolving along both neo-Darwinian and psychodynamic pathways, that have been created. These nonverbal patterns are, after all, the behavioral elements underlying perceptions/attributions of attunement, affect-sharing, empathy, trust, and a host of other clinically relevant features for the therapist focused on the dyad. These are developmentally framed behavioral elements that may be interpreted as reflective of affect states, attentional structure, and/or features of individual temperament or personality that are also relevant clinically.

This paper proceeds to consider the fundamental place of observation and description of the nonverbal in the work of the infant–parent psychotherapist. The need for appropriate classification schemes in psychology are considered, along with their challenges. Distinct levels of categorization bring advantages and disadvantages, and problems of interobserver reliability are encountered. Following an overview, the Kestenberg Movement Profile (Amighi et al. 1999, Kestenberg 1975) is described, as it is unique as a classification system anchored in Laban's categorizations (Laban 1966) and fundamentally linked to developmental and psychological processes and psychodynamic formulations.

Nonverbal Processes in Infant–Parent Psychotherapy

Observational skills are important tools in all domains of psychotherapy and psychoanalysis. How clinicians listen, and how they select what to respond to in traditional verbal therapies has spawned much literature, and points to multilayered influences, including theoretical orientation, personality of the therapist, and ongoing countertransferential phenomena. Particular observational opportunities are available, and skills called upon, in the special circumstance of infant–parent psychotherapy, where the baby's presence is such a central ingredient (Lieberman et al. 2000). What tools are therapist-observers to use, however, in the work of identifying individual and interactive themes, emotional states and developmental shifts? What is the relationship among what and how the therapist observes, the manner of the therapist's empathic attitude, and the potentiation of mutative change in the therapeutic process?

As Fraiberg (1980) had initially envisioned, the powerful influence of parental-representational "ghosts in the nursery" (Fraiberg et al. 1975) illuminates the manner of intergenerational transmission upon the infant, for example, how the parent's conflictual feelings regarding the baby are anchored in his or her own childhood experiences. Yet, while highlighting the power of a parent's newfound awareness of relevant childhood experiences in relating to an infant, Lieberman and colleagues (2000), and Lieberman and Zeanah (1999), among others, have clarified some of the limitations of insight-oriented verbal interpretive work in many contexts, highlighting instead the efficacy of nonspoken demonstrations of the therapist's empathic attitude and behavior toward parent and baby. When the circumstances of the families are particularly laden with stress, for example, impoverishment, the quality of the parent–therapist relationship has been considered especially primary, and the task of the therapist has been especially oriented toward attunement to the parents' immediate subjective experience. The therapist is certainly in a unique role, perhaps as one existing in the transitional space between infant and parent.

Infant–parent psychotherapies vary in method based on circumstance, orientation, and goals. These therapies differ, in part, in the degree to which clinical attention is focused on parental conflict, upon the connection between past and present that may be distorting the infant's selfhood in the eyes of caregivers, upon corrective attachment experiences facilitated by the therapeutic relationship, or upon more directive exercise of reciprocal and mutually regulated and gratifying forms of interaction (Lieberman et al. 2000, Stern 1995). Research involving careful observations of infants led to an enhanced appreciation of the baby's capacities and sense of agency (Stern 1985), and to a greater acknowledgment of the dyadic complexity of the parent–infant relationship when viewed in terms of the quality of mutually and reciprocally regulated experiences (Beebe et al. 1997, Tronick 1998). In fact, increased understandings of the nature of dyadic interchange between parent and infant, and more intricate views of how parent and infant mutually construct meanings, have increasingly influenced the wide body of psychoanalytic and developmental theories, while amplifying constructivist and relational thinking.

In their review of varied infant–parent programs, Lieberman and Zeanah (1999) consider the mutative factors operative in varied therapeutic approaches, such as group interventions and interaction guidance (McDonough 1993). Of significant consequence are the therapist's positive regard, attentiveness to the parent's needs, and empathic responsiveness. These researchers suggest that it is through a corrective attachment experience that the parent becomes able to change negative expectations to greater trust, and move increasingly toward mutuality and caring. The therapist must become a secure base (Bowlby 1988) through the utilization of therapeutic empathy. The mutual trust sought between the parent and child should be inherent in the working relationships that include the therapist. This is also aligned with Stern's (1995) framework, conceptualizing an open-system model of the infant–parent relationship, including constituent factors of the interactive behaviors of both infant and parent (hence, the external components of the relationship), and of the representations of both infant and parent (hence, the internal components of the relationship). An intervention addressing one component (e.g., the parent's representations) would likely affect the others as well.

Greenspan (1997) described particular "gestural challenges" potentially posed to therapists by patients of various ages, leading him to address the nonverbal communication and gestural negotiations that occur in the context of a therapeutic session. He suggests that the first goal of therapy involves the establishment (or reengagement) of clear, reciprocal, boundary-defining nonverbal communications, often addressing the developmental deficit in the earliest kind of gestural and interactive negotiations. Greenspan suggests that in the process of treatment it is the therapist who chooses how to "countergesture" in such a way that the patient's regulatory problems are addressed while maintaining the integrity of the gestural system and respecting the patient's individuality. I suggest that the infant–parent psychotherapist is involved in a complex process in choosing such countergestures, for they may carry multiple meanings. In the treatment of a regulatory-disordered child, a therapist's gesture may, in one instance, directly offer empathic understanding and yet containment and regulatory support for the child, while simultaneously supporting the parent's ability both to be contained and to similarly offer containment.

A major influence on theory and practice in infant mental health, and in infant–parent psychotherapy in particular, has been attachment theory (Bowlby 1988, Lieberman and Zeanah 1999), with its heightened concern for direct observation by the therapist, and for its focus on empathy and sensitive responsiveness. Attachment classifications have primarily been made through discriminating observations of the toddler's attachment strategies in a laboratory situation (Ainsworth et al. 1978, Lyons-Ruth and Jacobvitz 1999, Main and Solomon 1990). This research involves specific operationalizations of mostly nonverbal behavior, especially upon reunion, and insists on the attainment of intercoder agreement. As Solomon and George (1999) note, coding in the Strange Situation does not involve event recording, wherein predefined acts are minutely operationalized. Rather, a multidimensional, categorical template is described, and coders gain experience in placing newly seen behaviors within these templates. The behaviors observed are categorized without reference to any specific system of nonverbal analysis, but rather on agreed-upon gestures and features that allow for reliable differentiation by coders, and that have proven valid through an enormous body of research. Relevant infant/toddler behaviors for classification involve such features as smiling, seeking contact, exploring, seeking distance, visible distress, signs of angry rejection, failing to find comfort (Ainsworth et al. 1978), and/or regarding the disorganized/disoriented category, direct indications of fear/apprehension of a parent (Main and Solomon 1990).

An extension of such a template-driven classification scheme has been clinically applied in the recognition of disturbances and disorders of attachment. Zeanah and Boris (2000) note the challenges of developing clinic-based assessment methods of attachment, as it appears that the more structured research methods lack sufficient sensitivity for the clinician. Features such as "indiscriminate friendliness," "self-endangerment," "clinging/inhibited exploration," "vigilance/hypercompliance," and "role-reversal" are important patterns used for diagnostic differentiation of attachment disorders, and the nonverbal realm may be the primary channel of expression.

People vary greatly in their ability and style in capturing and documenting observed behaviors, and this is reflected in notably different narratives.[2] Stern (1995) notes that "any element of the clinical situation can be used as a privileged port of entry" (p. 131). Indeed, in referring to a case of an 18-month-old, using the interaction as the port of entry, Stern carefully describes the sequentially unfolding videotaped behavior of a child seeking his mother. Upon not attaining her in the manner he apparently wanted, the child showed a reactive microdepression. His vignette ably served to demonstrate the utility of using a videotape of mother–child interaction with the mother to elicit her relevant representations and memories. It is interesting to note Stern's (1995) descriptors in the following section of this vignette:

2. Along with Dr. Phyllis Ackman (see this issue), the author collaborates in training doctoral psychology students in infant/toddler–parent observation at Pace University. In this context, it is notable how equally attentive and thoughtful observers may nonetheless highlight different behaviors, and certainly use different adjectives or labels, in describing behaviors in their narratives that have implications for the attribution of meaning.

> He dragged a kiddie chair between mother and therapist, blocking their views of each other. He climbed upon the chair and reached his arms out toward his mother, indicating clearly that he wanted to be brought into her lap. She did not pick him up. Instead, she reached her arms out to him, the palms of her hands facing up. The infant, while standing on the chair, posed his hands, palm down, on her hands. She then simply led him by the hands off the chair down onto the floor and to the side. . . . The boy [after the mother resumed talking to her therapist] . . . let out a long breath and lowered his head. His posture crumbled, as if he were being deflated. . . . [p. 131]

Focusing on the descriptors themselves, Stern, certainly an endowed and seasoned observer, appeared to identify the child's arm gesture as carrying great expressive meaning and semiotic weight. Hence, he readily interprets its meaning directly, going on to describe the mother's gestural reply in terms that we recognize were not fulfilling of the young boy's inferred wish, ultimately leading to his plaintive posture. Such a style of description resonates with clinicians who similarly employ well-developed eyes for motivationally relevant cues and affectively relevant responses. The clinician in such a case is building upon his or her everyday ability to accurately note, and infer meaning from, nonverbal behavior. No special coding system or language of movement was actuated in Stern's observational and descriptive task. Yet, in all such descriptions a selection process is evident. Here, for instance, we don't read directly about the boy's facial gestures, or the mother's. The manners in which the chair got dragged and the climbing occurred are not elaborated. We hear of the directionality of the hands, but not of their state of tension. The "long breath" conveys a temporal quality of graduality or extended time, but there was no comment on the time dimension of other behaviors. When the boy's "posture crumbled" do we picture all planes (horizontal, vertical, and sagittal) equally involved in his becoming "deflated," or is one or another more primary? Of what relevance would such additional information be?

Classification Schemes in Psychology: Selecting Relevant Units of Behavior and Expression

Nonverbal behaviors are generally not subjected to a specific classification system, even when they serve as primary data for impressions influencing psychological theory building or clinical intervention (exceptions regarding the clinical situation include research by Davis and Hadicks 1994 and the recent psychoanalytic case studies of La Barre 2001). When language process is the focus of analysis in research and assessment, systematic approaches have evolved to classify statements within the large body of linguistic and semiotic studies. Hence, the systematic approach to assessing properties of discourse offered by Grice (1989), focusing on qualitative, quantitative, relational, and manneristic features of the language used, proved invaluable in the development of the highly fruitful Adult Attachment Interview (AAI) technique (Hesse 1999, Main 1991), which extended to appraisal of linguistic features bearing indication of psychological influences. For instance, "lapses in metacognitive monitoring" are seen as meaningful insofar as they convey something about an impact on working memory or consciousness triggered by discussion of traumatic events.

Much thought, examination, and selection had to precede operationalization of relevant behavioral units that might serve as relevant markers in AAI coding. Only then could behavioral units having less or no deemed predictive relevance be discarded. At once so distinct but nonetheless parallel, systematizers of the Rorschach, especially as integrated and extended by Exner (1993) evolved diagnostic approaches to the appraisal of perceptual processes, reflective of complex psychological functions elicited by specific visual stimuli. A selection process ensued, considering which perceptual process features proved indicative of personality-laden psychological processes. These were then incorporated into the interpretable structural summary, while other perceptual processes were not included.

In everyday clinical work, an individual's use of language or perceptual processes are grist for the mill of "clinical impression." In fact, the experienced clinician who is also an AAI interviewer and scorer is likely to listen with an enhanced third ear. The clinician who is proficient at projective techniques is likely sensitized to relevant perceptual and associative processes shared by a patient in therapy. What overarching classifications of nonverbal behaviors are currently available to empirically study infant–parent dyadic process, as well as to sharpen the observational skills of the therapist?

Nonverbal Patterns and Their Description: From the Tavistock Model to The Neo-Darwinian Coding of Affect

The domains of "movement studies," "nonverbal communication," and "nonverbal behavior" are large and complex fields of study, each with its own history, having distinctive roots in the domains of anthropology, sociology, psychology, neuropsychology, psychiatry, biology/ethology, semiotics, and dance. As the multidisciplinary study of nonverbal actions unfolded, Davis (1979) astutely discriminated among systems using different levels of analysis, each applying distinct descriptive or coding lexicons; for example, some were derived from everyday action language, others from the discipline of linguistics, and still others from an interpretive framework.

The training and clinical usefulness of in vivo close observation in early childhood has become more widely appreciated, at least within developmental psychoanalysis (Bick 1964, Coll 2000, Miller et al. 1989, Reid 1997, Russell et al. 1995). Following the Bick/Tavistock model, students in the participant-observer role find that their empathy and sensitivity to nonverbal cues are essential components[3] in the process of deriving meaningful impressions, and that a seminar group serves as a container for the observers' emotional experiences. The descriptive narratives written attend closely to nonverbal phenomena but do not employ a predetermined lexicon or system. Hence, the Miller and colleagues (1989) text finds attribution-laden descriptors of babies such as "trying to escape," "coping through absorption," "not communicating any feeling very strongly," "absorbed in," "insistent," and "complaining." Similarly, descriptors of parents include "preoccupied with guilt," "lack of warmth and intimacy," "great regret," and "fleetingly in contact with painful or depressed feelings." The attributional nature of such descriptions does not itself diminish their potential for accuracy, but in offering impressionistic interpretations, the raw descriptive level is left to the observer to be internally processed. Participant-observers pay exquisite attention to their own inner processes because they are acknowledging of the mediating role their own processes play. In a clinical or dynamic observing context, as framed by the Tavistock Model (e.g., Alvarez and Furgiuele 1997, Wittenberg 1997) the psychodynamic observer or therapist may find it useful to maintain a high degree of cognizance of his or her attributions to the parent and child so as to heighten awareness of the affective exchanges, and to closely monitor feelings arising in him-

3. The experiences of psychoanalysts pursuing specialized training in parent–infant psychotherapy at the New York Freudian Society, under the tutelage of Dr. Anni Bergman and colleagues, certainly bear out the importance of the observational experience, narrative writing, and seminar containment.

or herself for appraisal of transference and countertransference happenings in the clinical process. However, these labels nonetheless derive from some amalgam of clinical and everyday languages, and the attributions invariably bear some aspects of the attributor. The clinical reader of observation-narratives are influenced by such attributions.

As the use of video technology has progressed alongside a growing respect for the importance, albeit of a subtle and complex nature, of parent–infant interaction patterns (e.g., Beebe 1998, Cohen and Beebe 2002, Zelenko and Benham 2000), there still remain significant differences as to the nature of description observers apply. Nonverbal researchers have long struggled with problems inherent in raw data collection (e.g., Hirsbrunner et al. 1987); some descriptors may be so global as to lose meaningfulness, and some may be so minute or complex as to defy reliable notation. Technology, in the forms of computer event-recording and extreme slow-motion and frame-by-frame sequencing helps tackle some of the complexity factors, but it may do so at the expense of clinical utility and overall practicality of application. Perhaps the more important questions remain as to which level(s) of analysis and which framework(s) for coding offer data that can be meaningfully and validly interpreted.

We have learned that much can be ascertained from attributions of affect, as reflected by research employing the IFEEL Pictures (Emde et al. 1993), in which adult subjects are asked to label the primary feeling expressed by standardized infant pictures, based on static nonverbal features. Emde (1993) proffers a rationale for the method, within a developmental systems theoretical orientation involving affect exchange in interaction. As Szajnberg (1993) demonstrates in a study utilizing the IFEEL pictures as stimuli for projective stories, different experiences with infants are likely to lead to different attributions. (In the case of his study, qualitative aspects of projective stories differentiated mothers of preterms from mothers of full-terms.)

Perspectives on classifying nonverbal indices of emotion vary, in part, upon theoretical views as to whether emotion is understood to operate dimensionally or categorically/discretely (Izard 1993). Differentiation theory posits that experience and learning build upon two or three original dimensions (e.g., hedonic tone and physiological activation) in the development of more specific emotions, whereas differential theory suggests an innateness to emotional response schemas. Galati and Lavelli (1997) found that when adults were asked to view neonate and infant videotaped facial expressions, they more readily agreed as to the signaling of activation and pleasure/displeasure than they were able to offer verbal ascriptions regarding the situation or more specific emotion, and that agreement improved as the child aged in the first few months of life. The categories generated by Darwin's (1872) brilliant and meticulous observations of emotions (e.g., joy, surprise, anger, fear, sadness, disgust, interest), further promoted by Tomkins (1962) as essential to adaptation, and by Ekman and Friesen (1978) and Izard (1982) as biologically anchored and fairly universal, have the advantage of being reasonably operationalized. This body of literature conceives of unique organizing and motivational functions of discrete emotions (Izard 1993). Fridlund and colleagues (1987) noted that universality was demonstrated for expressions of happiness, anger, disgust, sadness, and combined fear/surprise. These authors gave thoughtful consideration to the difficult issue of choosing the appropriate behavioral units to study and label in their facial coding systems. This broadly coherent line of conceptualization gave rise to Izard's tools for coding infant emotions, namely the Maximally Descriptive Facial Movement Coding system (MAX; Izard 1979) and the System for Identifying Affect Expression by Holistic Judgment (AFFEX; Izard and Dougherty 1980). Applying the MAX, Termine and Izard (1988), finding further support for Izard's differential emotions theory, demonstrated that 9-month-old boys and girls show longer gaze and express more joy when mothers express joy, and they express more sadness, anger, and gaze aversion when mothers show more sadness.

Ekman and Friesen (1978), focusing primarily on adult expressions, developed the Facial Action Coding System (FACS), anchored in the anatomic specificity of those muscle combinations resulting in visibly distinct facial actions. The 44 discriminated action units, singly or in combination, basically account for all visible facial movement. Oster and Rosenstein (see Oster et al. 1997) developed and applied the Baby FACS, with action units, coding intensities, and variations in smiling and negative affect expressions derived from observed facial expressions in infants. Oster and colleagues showed that the basic repertoire of infant facial expressions is evidently preserved even in infants with severe craniofacial anomalies.

Hence a large body of research has accumulated that verifies the utility of categorizing nonverbal, facial-muscle components of affect expression. The ethogrammatic measurement tools that have evolved clarify those features that are most relevant in the information exchange in which affect is signaled, received, and labeled by the receiver. It appears that we can think of the action units incorporated into these measures as carrying meaning, and that this meaning is significantly primed in biology.

As the communicative process of nonverbal expression and recognition/attribution is dyadic, we also note that the receiver can misunderstand or distort the meaning of the sender; either a baby or a parent can misread or miscue the other. Recognition/attribution skills are variable, as reflected by the extreme deficits demonstrated in individuals manifesting nonverbal learning disability (NLD) (Rourke 1989). Duke and Nowicki (1996) have addressed some of the features and possible remedies for the child with "dyssemia" (their term for the relative inability to accurately interpret nonverbal cues). Observers of early dyadic processes would likely implicate proclivities for miscuing and misreading in the infant–parent exchange as heightening the risk of later difficulties comprehending nonverbal behavior, especially in light of the importance of the emotional referencing process (Emde and Sorce 1983).

NONVERBAL BEHAVIORS AS LIKELY MEDIATORS OF INTERGENERATIONAL TRANSMISSION

As psychodynamic developmentalist thinking has focused on representational structures fundamental to interpersonal behavior (Bowlby 1988, Fonagy 1994, Main et al. 1985, Sandler and Sandler 1978, Tronick and Cohn 1989), a clearer picture has emerged regarding how self- and other-representations serve to regulate a young child's interactive behavior with a caregiver. Furthermore, the work utilizing the Adult Attachment Interview (Hesse 1999, Van Ijzendoorn 1995) demonstrates that parental mental representations stemming from the parent's own childhood have determining influences upon the child's security of attachment. Moreover, intersubjectivity emerges as self- and other-representations are to some degree overlapping, and moments (varying in quality and duration) of affect sharing wax and wane. Implicit is the idea that nonverbal processes are pivotal in the dynamic conveyance of both child and caregiver experiences to and from each other. The term *mirroring* and/or the success or failure of the *mirroring function* have become ways of describing co-occurring infant–parent behaviors that serve identificatory processes and the creation of self–other boundaries. While this mirroring function is interconnected with internal representational experience, the observing researcher or clinician may differ greatly in the focus and framing of which nonverbal behaviors are being mirrored. Anatomically, is it the hand, the arm, the face, or possibly a posture? Is it the change of tension, change of shape, manner of gesture, facial configuration, or already symbolized sign that is being mirrored? On what basis do we determine whether the behavior primarily conveys affect (and, if so, might it be the hedonic tone or the interpersonal comfort level that is mirrored)?

Jointly Constructed Moment-By-Moment Relatedness

Stern (1995) posits that even for the young infant, events have temporal contours that themselves allow affective experience to be represented. Acutely focused on mostly nonverbal happenings, he describes the "feeling shapes" of subjective experiences that result in the structuring of time, and that allow for affective experience to gain internal representation. Stern's concept of the "proto-narrative envelope" refers to the narrative-like structure of the baby's enacted motive and the interpersonal experience of the moment, which helps clarify a given infant's way-of-being with his or her parent. An informed, sensitive, and reflective therapist might utilize careful observation to form imagined representations of the infant that become ports of entry. A question raised in this paper is whether systematic ways of observing qualitative aspects of the behaviors themselves help inform the therapist/observer about such representations.

Beebe and colleagues (2000) have looked further at the way temporal patterns (e.g., pauses, interruptions, turntaking, rate, etc.) are coordinated in the organization of social relatedness. They note that both vocal and kinesic infant–adult dialogue are bidirectionally coordinated, and that the coordination of timing patterns operates through expectancies. Patterns of expectation are used to define presymbolic representation in the first year. Beebe and colleagues specifically found that level of vocal-rhythm coordination at 4 months of age predicted security-of-attachment status at 12 months. It was the midrange of coordination, conceptualized as reflecting optimum flexibility and variability, that predicted secure attachment, whereas the highest degree of vocal rhythm coordination predicted insecure infant attachment (disorganized and anxious-resistant), and the lowest degree also predicted insecurity (avoidant). Hence, Beebe and colleagues note that it is not the fact of bidirectinoal regulation that is predictive, but it is the degree of coordination.

Movement Patterns, Affect, and Dyadic Interaction at the Crossroads of Developmental Neurobiology

Current developmental neurobiology recognizes the importance of experience-dependent synaptogenesis (Greenough and Black 1992, Nelson 2000), in which there is a renewed appreciation for early psychological influences, in this case upon the pruning of neurological connections that uniquely give shape to an individual's neuroarchitecture and related self-attributes. The brain is influenced by, and is influencing of, experience. It is said of both the infant (Stern 1985, 1995) and of the brain (Berthoz 2000), that each seeks to predict and create, and that this is done by developing internal models of the world, that is, of the environment, of significant others, and of the body. Schore (1997) has advanced the idea that attunement interactions between baby and caregiver involve right-brain to right-brain communication, especially implicating the orbitofrontal cortex, postulating that these early attunement/attachment experiences play important roles in fostering the ultimate brain circuitry that takes shape. Schore reasons that abuse, neglect, and chronic states of misattunement create an impaired ability to regulate stress-related emotions due to an over-pruning of synapses. The complexities bearing on exactly how synaptogenic and neuroendocrine consequences of experience are demonstrated in particularized movement patterns have not yet been studied.

The fine-grained movement analyses of Bernstein (1967) anchored the more recent neurointegrative conceptualizations of Berthoz (2000), who addresses how motor synergies (understood as perceptuomotor actions) form the basis of movement and point to the complex way in which contiguous neurons control a repertoire of actions. These also control internal simulations of movement, which he variously terms *schemas* or *kinesthetic series*. Berthoz notes that movement, as in the direction of gaze in parent–infant interaction, is an integral part of perception. Berthoz suggests that a coherent evaluation of people is dependent on the ability to evaluate the relationship between one's own body and the environment (further hypothesizing that autistic children's interpersonal deficits are related to deficiencies in their coding of space).

Contributions of the Kestenberg Frame to the Goals and Methods of Infant–Parent Psychotherapy

Through the KMP and related perspectives on nonverbal behavior, Kestenberg (1975, 1985a,b, Sossin 1999a, Sossin and Loman 1992) contributed a tool of nonverbal/movement observation that potentially equips the infant–parent therapist to appraise arenas of attunement and clashing, matching and mismatching, and other harmonic and discordant patterns. The KMP scheme for cataloguing movement patterns drew upon the choreographer Rudolf Laban's (1960, 1966, Bartenieff and Lewis 1980) system of dance notation and movement analysis, and reflects the influence of the work of Paul Schilder (1935, Kestenberg 1985a). Child and parent observations utilizing the KMP led to developmental and psychological elaborations. Through individual or dyadic profiling, or more impressionistically, by "seeing" within the KMP framework, the therapist can focus on nonverbal patterns as meaningful indices of drive, affect, defense, adaptation, feelings about oneself and about others, as well as about empathy and trust.

In a series of papers, Kestenberg and Buelte (1977a,b, 1983) carefully examined the analogs of qualitative motor expression, infant experience in the infant–caregiver context, and processes identifiable in adult psychotherapeutic and psychoanalytic treatment. Kestenberg (1985b) continued this thesis in her delineation of the flow of empathy and trust in the infant–parent relationship, underscoring the distinctions between disturbances in empathy and breaches in trust. Buelte (1992) described an approach of "movement retraining" for infants and adults focused on movement patterns deemed phase appropriate in the service of mastering phase-specific developmental tasks.

Rich approaches to intervention, directly utilizing movement observation and facilitated movement experiences with infants and toddlers, have evolved within dance/movement therapy (Tortora 1994). The significance and specific utility of the KMP framework in the field of dance/movement therapy has been detailed by Lewis (1984, 1993), Loman (1994) and Loman and Merman (1996).

Kestenberg and colleagues further observed motor patterns to lend insight into the psychological understanding of many developmentally relevant phenomena, as in their considerations of self- and object-representations (Kestenberg 1971), the development of paternal attitudes (Kestenberg et al. 1982), pregnancy (Kestenberg 1980), preoedipal phase development (Kestenberg 1982), fetal experience (Kestenberg 1987), early bonding (Kestenberg 1990), parent–child holding patterns (Romer and Sossin 1990), narcissism and earliest experiences (Kestenberg and Borowitz 1990), the impact of developmental disabilities on the evolving sense of self (Sossin 1993), and aggression (Kestenberg et al. 1993). Sossin and Loman (1992) described some clinical applications of the KMP, and this was furthered by Loman (1995) in her case study of the application of the KMP to autism. Despite the broad spectrum of these endeavors, the KMP work has largely remained unintegrated into psychodynamically informed models of infant–parent psychotherapy (Sossin 1999a).

OUTLINE OF THE KMP

A complete KMP of a single subject classifies movement patterns into, minimally, 62 codable patterns, further coded for additional features that raise the total number of distinctly quantified movement variables over 100. Many ratios and equations are derived from the raw data. The codable patterns are organized into nine clusters, eight of which will be concisely reviewed here. Developmental, theoretical, notational, and procedural factors, along with issues pertaining to context, reliability and validity, and specialized applications, are detailed in the work of Amighi and colleagues (1999).

The place of the KMP notator resembles that of the closely observing infant–parent therapist, calling upon the attainment of kinesthetic identification/attunement with both the infant and the parent "objectively" observed, while self-reflectively alert to sources of interference that distort this identification and the accuracy of perception. The long course of study and practice leading to reliable KMP notation[4] involves gaining mastery of the knowledge base of the multiple movement factors and their distinct operationalizations, and the conceptual framework that incorporates the developmental and dynamic interrelations of individual movement factors with others. Infant–parent therapists attending to the nonverbal must not only have access to the psychological self-knowledge that allows for inner access to countertransference feelings, but also access to their own movement repertoire, so that notational interferences are readily recognized.

The following material offers a synopsis of KMP movement factors that might be informative to the clinician appraising or intervening with an infant–parent dyad. Figure 1 shows a skeleton of major movement factors incorporated into the KMP.

4. KMP training usually involves approximately 80 hours of class or individual instruction to learn the notational system and begin to apply it . Many more hours and multiple experiences of observation, notation, data computation, and profile construction are required before reliability can be attained, and further collaborative experience is required in the acquisition of interpretive skills.

Figure 1. Brief Outline of the Kestenberg Movement Profile (KMP)

The following chart labels some of the principal movement factors applied in the KMP, with polar descriptors listed across from one another. The italicized terms occupy plot points in the quantified and graphic KMP. Descriptive words listed alongside Tension-Flow Attributes and Shape-Flow Attributes are meant as suggestive and descriptive, and not as inclusive or providing a basis for interpretation. Tension-Flow/Effort patterns are grouped with the Shape-Flow/Shaping patterns that are conceived to provide them with specific structure, potentiating "matching." Neither Tension-Flow Rhythms nor Shape-Flow-Design patterns are included below.

Tension-Flow Attributes

FreeFlow (lack of restraint)	Bound Flow (inhibition)
Adjustment of Tension Flow (affect modulation)	*Even Level of Tension* (indifference, sameness)
Low Intensity of Tension (low degree of feeling)	*High Intensity of Tension* (high degree of feeling)
Gradual Change of Tension (patience, deliberateness)	*Abrupt Change of Tension* (impulsivity, quickness)

Neutral Flow of Tension (loss of elasticity, deanimation)

Shape-Flow Attributes (Bipolar patterns are differentiated from unipolar patterns)

Growing (comfort, approach)	Shrinking (discomfort, withdrawal)
Widening (Horizontal expansion)	*Narrowing* (Horizontal constriction)
Lengthening (Vertical, becoming bigger)	*Shortening* (Vertical, becoming smaller)
Bulging (Sagittal, feeling full)	*Hollowing* (Sagittal emptying)

Neutral Shape (loss of plasticity and loss of structure)

Precursors of Effort

(Reflective of learning modes/drive-related defenses)

Flexibility	*SPACE*	*Channeling*
Gentleness	*WEIGHT*	*Straining/Vehemence*
Hesitation	*TIME*	*Suddenness*

Directions in Space

(Using two dimensions, expressive of object related learning/defenses)

Moving Sideways	*HORIZONTAL*	*Moving Across the Body*
Moving Upward	*VERTICAL*	*Moving Downward*
Moving Forward	*SAGITTAL*	*Moving Backward*

Figure 1. *(continued)*

Effort

(Reflecting manners of coping with forces of external reality)

Indirectness	*SPACE*	*Directness*
Lightness	*WEIGHT*	*Strength*
Deceleration	*TIME*	*Acceleration*

Shaping of Space in Planes

(Using three dimensions, expressive of multifaceted relationships)

Spreading	*HORIZONTAL*	*Enclosing*
Ascending	*VERTICAL*	*Descending*
Advancing	*SAGITTAL*	*Retreating*

This outline is derived in part from Kestenberg (1985b). The reader is referred to Amighi and colleagues (1999) for a more complete description of the KMP method, including a fuller description of movement terms, relevant ratios, equations, and other quantitative factors pertaining to profiling and interpreting KMP data. It has been posited that there is a developmental ascendency from top to bottom. Tension-Flow/Effort pertains to drives, hedonic affects defenses against drives and ego-adaptations, organized in terms of movements linked to space, weight, and time. Shape-Flow/Shaping patterns pertain to self and relationships, and are organized in terms of the prominence of horizontal, vertical, and sagittal dimensional/planar aspects of the movements. Patterns on the left of each diagram are affined with free flow and growing and those on the right of each diagram are affined with bound flow and shrinking.

FLOW FACTORS

From the beginning, an infant demonstrates some degree of regulation of *tension-flow* and *shape-flow*. Tension-flow refers to rhythmic changes in muscle tension, dimensionalized as continuously shifting between relative degrees of *free-flow* and *bound-flow*. Free-flow refers to movement that is the product of agonist muscle action with little opposition, producing less unrestrained patterns, whereas bound-flow refers to movement that results from the co-contraction of the antagonist muscle along with the agonist, producing more constrained patterns. *Animated-flow* ranges across high and low intensities, but maintains vivified elasticity, often in support of alert and actively engaged activities. When elasticity is significantly reduced, *neutral-flow* appears. A depressed mother may show a disproportionate degree of neutral flow in her facial expressions, bodily states, or holding patterns. Though the baby may attempt to reanimate the mother, the baby may resort to attuning with her within this deanimated, minimally changing flow property. Such flow-interchanges are bidirectional and the dyadic experience is coconstructed. Such occurrences may be relatively fleeting in the case of microdepressions, but more frequent and lasting in the midst of more significant stress or psychopathology. Tension-flow is notated in controlled but free-form tracings, and these are labeled in terms of both *tension-flow rhythms* and *tension-flow attributes*.

Shape-flow pertains to the ongoing *growing* and *shrinking* of bodily dimensions. With breathing as a prototype, growing patterns are naturally related to inhalation and opening up, and shrinking with exhalation and closing oneself off. Though shape-flow is continuously and rhythmically changing like tension-flow, it cannot be notated in a continuous fashion as yet because the methodologies are two-dimensional and the phenomenon is three-dimensional. Hence, an effort/shape Laban-derived notational procedure was extrapolated, notating ongoing changes in shape-flow across horizontal, vertical, and sagittal dimensions, distinguishing symmetric *bipolar shape-flow* actions from asymmetric *unipolar shape-flow* actions.

Tension-Flow Rhythms

Among the movement patterns incorporated into the KMP, those associated with eight of the clusters follow an organization developmentally linked to Laban's conceptualizations of effort and shape (Bartenieff and Lewis 1980, Laban and Lawrence 1947). The exception is the cluster called *tension-flow rhythms,* referring to recognizable ways in which muscle tension periodically alternates between relative free and bound flow. These recognizable patterns were deemed by Kestenberg (1975) to be in the service of "drives" as she recast them against the backdrop of a psychosexual phase theory that was revised largely on the basis of such observations of the nonverbal.[5] *Pure rhythms,* originally associated with phase-specific functions, are differenti-

5. Kestenberg perceived significant deficiencies with psychoanalytic drive theory. As numerous psychoanalysts abandoned drive theory, she went about trying to revise it by incorporating developmentally relevant observations, by expecting a multiplicity of drives to be present in each developmental phase, by bringing attention to urethral and inner-genital phases, and by emphasizing the nature of libidinal and sadistic subphases. Tension-flow alternations were identifiable as libidinal or sadistic versions of oral, anal, urethral, inner-genital, or phallic rhythms (or a blending of one or more). As Prince (2001) implies, this attempt at revision may have isolated Kestenberg as a theorist, as her revisions were welcomed neither by traditionalists nor by those finding little use for drive theory. This isolation may have contributed to a reticence to attend to the nonverbal as she fashioned it.

ated from *mixed rhythms,* which may be adaptive or derailing, as they modify pure rhythms reflecting individual personality characteristics. These rhythms were originally named in accordance with the phase-dominant drives they were theoretically linked to (Kestenberg and Sossin 1979) and later named more descriptively (Amighi et al. 1999).

As tension-flow rhythms are synchronized between mother and infant, *attunement* emerges. Needs and feelings are responsively duplicated on the level of physical sensation (Loman 1994). Attunement of tension-flow rhythms serves feelings of sameness, while clashing rhythms serve differentiation between self and other. Ergo, optimal degrees of parent–infant attunement change through the course of development.

Tension-Flow Attributes

Conceived of as mood-regulating mechanisms, tension-flow attributes are not themselves affects. Rather they reflect manners of change in the rise and fall of tension (elasticity); they are the medium of the expression of affects of pleasure and displeasure (Sossin 1999b). "Fighting" attributes are differentiated from "indulging" attributes; thus even-flow is differentiated from flow adjustment, high intensity, from low intensity and abrupt from gradual.

Bipolar Shape-Flow

As manifestations of plasticity, bipolar shape-flow refers to symmetrical expansions and contractions. These are linked to affective relations to stimuli and objects in the environment. An infant will show bipolar growing patterns when comfortable with environmental provisions like warmth, and will show bipolar shrinking patterns when in discomfort, as when it is too cold. Growing movements expose the baby to the environment, while shrinking movements reduce exposure. Developing trust, stability, and confidence are served by bipolar shape-flow.

Unipolar Shape-Flow

Growing unilaterally when approaching an attractive stimulus and shrinking unilaterally in withdrawal from a noxious stimulus reflect unipolar shape-flow patterns. Like other flow-based factors, these pertain to affective experience but also to feelings associated with attraction/repulsion or approach/withdrawal patterns that may be particularly reflective of responsivity to caregiving. As bipolar shape-flow contributes to stability, unipolar shape-flow contributes to mobility.

Precursors of Effort

Though involved in attempts to cope with elements of space, weight, and time, precursors of effort (or pre-efforts) do not subordinate the role of tension-flow attributes. Thus, they involve moving with or against environmental elements without mastery, and with a more prominent affect-laden quality. Actions involved in learning, as well as defensive maneuvers, show greater use of precursors of effort. A mother worried about placing her child in a new play environment may put her child down with bound flow, gentleness (involving low intensity), channeling (involving even-flow), and hesitation (involving graduality). When more confident, this mother will likely use the related effort qualities, and the tension-flow attributes will be far less participatory.

In infant–parent psychotherapy, the therapist may particularly note, through observations of such precursors of effort, that confidence and mastery in particular activities are neither demonstrated by the mother nor developing in the child. A mother may be conscious of the goal-oriented task at hand (e.g., changing a diaper, supporting sitting or standing, feeding), yet may be quite involved in a bidirectional process of affect sharing in which uncertainty and anxiety are excessive. These movement qualities, when beyond the scope of the learning curve for a new task (reflected by child or parent), cue the therapist to a potential port of entry. The style of the intervention can range, depending on the ongoing orientation applied, from using the observation as a stimulus for the mother's associations and remembering, to direct modeling, to guidance incorporating support around tasks eliciting her lowered confidence, and to direct movement interventions.

Shaping in Directions

There is a developmental progression from unipolar shape-flow to shaping in directions. Simple pointing movements (e.g., pointing sideways or across, up or down, forward or backward) emerge alongside both interpersonal and cognitive developments, but the functions of such directional movements can include localizing objects in space, defending against objects in the environment, labeling and defining, creating bridges to interpersonal relationships, as well as gesturally facilitating thought and language.

Efforts

Maturing upon the groundwork of tension-flow attributes and pre-efforts, efforts are movement patterns demonstrating effective coping with external reality, differentiated among the space, weight, and time dimensions of the environment. There is a parallel developmental progression between space, weight, and time efforts and a focus on attention and interest in where things are, to the development of intentionality and interest in what things are, to the development of decision-making skills and an awareness of when things happen.

Shaping in Planes

Whereas a directional movement moves along a spoke- or arc-like vector in a spatial dimension, the concave and convex movements included in shaping in planes traverse at least two dimensions, generally carving space elliptically. Each plane is conceived to have a primary and a secondary dimension. As understood and operationalized, spreading and enclosing are horizontal but they always include the sagittal dimension; ascending and descending are vertical but involve the horizontal dimension, and while advancing and retreating are sagittal, they are also vertical. The KMP literature (Amighi et al. 1999) suggests that these "sculpting" movements serve such behavioral patterns as exploration, confrontation, and anticipation, as well as corresponding to multidimensional representations of others, complexity of relationships, and social intelligence.

Complexity Factors

In KMP construction, *load-factors* (LFs) are percentages determined for each cluster, reflecting the frequency with which movement elements within a cluster appear alone or in combination with other such movement elements. Another KMP statistic is the *gain–expense ratio*, which reflects the degree to which movement attributes or elements of a given cluster appear relative to the number of flow-factor changes, at least one meaning of which pertains to affective control. Other statistical indices and additional features of the KMP approach to nonverbal behavior are not included here, such as the effects of culture and context, body-attitude, shape-flow-design patterns, gestural and postural movements, diagnostic and dynamically interpretive signifiers, developmental expectations, various applications, and so on. (The reader can refer to primary sources and the text by Amighi et al. 1999.)

Intrapersonal and Interpersonal Affinities, Clashes, Matches and Mismatches

This brief survey, while introducing the major movement patterns classified in the KMP, does not attempt to address the complex ways in which these movement patterns are understood to relate to each other, not only in interaction with others, but within one's own movement repertoire or in one's combination or phrasing of patterns. For instance, indirectness is "consonant" (i.e., affined) with free-flow and "dissonant" (i.e., clashing) with bound-flow, yet each combination occurs readily. Moreover, the shape-flow/shaping patterns provide structure for the tension-flow effort patterns; for example, bipolar hollowing is "matched" with abruptness with bound-flow, but of course can happen with graduality (a "mismatch"). These intrapersonal matches and mismatches lead evaluators using the KMP for interpretation purposes to comment on conflicts between different aspects of personality, or between affects of pleasure-displeasure and affects of comfort-discomfort. In an infant–parent couple, one can also see that certain parental shape-flow/shaping patterns offer externalized structure for the experiences of need and emotion on the part of the infant. Some combinations are more harmonious and others more discordant, and these too become ports of entry for the therapist.

Disorders of Attachment, Disorders of Empathy, and Disorders of Trust: Potential Applications of Classificatory Approaches to Nonverbal Behavior

Some infant–parent psychotherapy addresses problems in the child's relationship with primary attachment figures. These disorders of attachment were delineated by Zeanah and Boris (2000, also Lieberman and Zeanah 1995), and classified as disorders of nonattachment (with emotional withdrawal or indiscriminate sociability), attachment disorders (with self-endangerment, clinging/inhibited exploration, vigilance/hypercompliance, or role-reversal), and disrupted attachment disorder (evoked by sudden loss).

Diagnostically, dyadic parent–infant couples can usefully be subcategorized in terms of the manner in which they characteristically harmonize and in terms of the manner in which they tend to operate in disharmony. These "manners" are labeled in the KMP and further grouped into developmentally meaningful KMP clusters. Within a cluster, a parent and an infant may show similarities of tension-level, but differences in the way in which tension changes; or they may, for instance, share the way in which their shape-flow alters in the vertical dimension, but not in the sagittal or horizontal dimensions.

Kestenberg (1985a) defined empathy in kinesthetic terms as a "capacity to know another person's inner feelings, based on sensory experiences. . . . Empathy utilizes attunement in tension flow, which is based on kinesthetic identification with the tension changes of another person" (p. 162). To know how the child feels, the parent must attune to the child's patterns and resonate with them; the baby's feeling of "resonance" is what allows the baby to accept the parents' lead in altering the tension-flow patterns.[6] In analyzing a comforting sequence, Kestenberg (1985a) clarified that attunement on the part of the caregiver is not sufficient; rather, clashing is an essential part of the interaction in which a mother may calm a baby, but through the selection of patterns by the mother and the experience of resonance, one partner follows the other, leading to the reestablishment of attunement: "A feeling of sameness is recreated that is an intrinsic aspect of empathy" (p. 141).

By identifying the importance of clashing and the reinstatement of harmony, Kestenberg's ideas are comparable with those of Gianino and Tronick (1988, cf. Beebe and Lachmann 1994), who highlight the process of "disruption and repair of expected interactions." They underscore the formative importance of the dyad's ability to recoup from normally occurring breaches of attunement (as in compatible tension-flow) and of adjustment (as in compatible shape-flow). These are conceptually akin to the repair of empathic ruptures and to the repair of moments of mistrust. The latter involves greater intersubjectivity alongside the infant's evolving schema-of-being-with (Stern 1995) that is augmented by predictable repair in interactive shape-flow matching, often creating a facilitated pathway from the infant's experiences of discomfort (shrinking shape-flow patterns, as in bipolar narrowing) to experiences of comfort (growing shape flow patterns, as in bipolar widening).

6. Kestenberg (1985a) drew upon the concept of resonance as it exists in music and voice to extend it to the *parent–infant* context of mutual processes. As the vehicle for empathy and attunement in ongoing interaction, Kestenberg introduced the concept of resonance to address the process of change (such as increasing or decreasing intensity) in the ongoing interaction. Resonance captured the process by which, for example, a mother would step away from (or out of) sameness with the baby's flow, leading the baby to follow suit, which reestablishes harmony at a slightly different level.

Regarding trust, Kestenberg (1985a) suggests: "the apparatus of shape flow is the conveyor of trust in the environment. It is the foremost vehicle of relatedness to others. . . . (it) has many functions that all are programmed for interaction" (p. 143). In reference to the coordination of tension-flow and shape-flow in breathing, for instance, Kestenberg notes: "the transmission of tension flow helps us to experience the feeling tones that go with respiration; the transmission of shape flow allows us to interpret these feelings and develop trust in ourselves and others" (p. 144). Within the KMP model, the infant's capacity for trust evolves from his or her expectation that discomfort will be followed by assuagement and comfort. Discomfort that is too impinging for too long, without relief, leads to a loss of trust.

The KMP framework emphasizes the importance of "phrasing" as a time structure, incorporating rhythm- and action-sequences into uniphasic or multiphasic orderings of movement patterns. The infant–parent psychotherapist can usefully examine the characteristic phrasing of both child and adult to find out when (e.g., in the introduction, main theme, transition or ending of characteristic phrases) various harmonies or clashes are more likely to occur. The interactive phrasing of one parent and child may typically achieve a reasonable degree of harmony in the main themes of phrases, yet just as typically get derailed in a manner of disjunction (or disengagement) accompanying transitions. Alternatively, a different parent–infant couple may transit well into co-action, but too rarely match in their main theme patterns.

As a way of seeing and assessing, the KMP may be of particular use to the infant–parent therapist by providing a means of identifying specific moments, reflective of "ways-of-being-with" that, drawing upon Stern (1995), allow special ports of entry into the experiential worlds of infant and parent. The raw data of movement patterns of infant and parent inform the diagnostician and therapist about patterns and phrasing. Seligman (2000) stresses the role of the interviewer in observing infant–parent interaction, taking note of qualities such as "characteristic rhythms, patterns of expectancy . . . characteristic affects . . . comfortable emotional flow and sense of efficacy and coordination" (p. 217), among others. Attention to such sometimes nuanced nonverbal patterns amidst the "buzz" of dyadic interaction can benefit from a lexicon that lends focus to meaningful signifiers. The KMP catalogues various patterns of animation and responsivity as well as interactive patterns that might simultaneously involve attunement and clashing. In broad outline, the mother who adjusts to the infant with corresponding shape-flow may engender the development of a certain predictability and *trust*; yet this may be in the absence of attunement in tension-flow, conveying (via this model) a lack of *empathy*. Similarly, resonating tension-flow may communicate corresponding feeling states in the absence of matching adjustments of shape-flow, hence producing an interactive state with empathy but without trust.

There are advantages to videotaping ongoing behavior between parent and child in the early phases of assessment and/or intervention. As other authors have found (e.g., Cohen and Beebe, in press, Stern 1995, Zelenko and Benham 2000), there may be utility in sharing video material with a parent for evocative or educative purposes (though one must be cautious in appraising the appropriateness of such use in light of the quality of the alliance with the parent and the state of ongoing transferences). The therapist can use his or her knowledge of the infant's movements to demonstrate the infant's motoric, regulatory, and interactive capacities, helping the parent to know the infant better, thereby helping to alter the parent's representation of the child. In this manner, the use of formalized observation of nonverbal patterns, as with the KMP, can build upon other approaches that utilize assessment of the baby to expand and in some cases rectify the parent's representation of the child (e.g., Brazelton 1992).

The dynamic infant–parent therapist can use the interpretive value of the KMP, in addition to more usual verbal techniques, to enter through the parent's representations. In fact, the fullest use of the KMP allows the therapist to work on multiple therapeutic targets, helping the parent to see herself as a better-able parent (her own self-representation), and simultaneously to help her see her child's resources more clearly. Such methods can take full advantage of insight and historically relevant verbal modalities in addition to the focus on nonverbal behavior. The goals in a particular case, wherein the infant may be showing an insecure, or perhaps disorganized attachment style, may include helping the mother, for instance, to come to terms with harm and disappointments from her past.

CONCLUSION

Essentially, all clinicians involved in appraising affects, motives, and states of mind rely to some degree (as mother regarding her baby) on their own abilities to read nonverbal behavior. An amalgam of sensitivity, empathy, intuition, and often unexplicated kinesthetic awareness operates to transpose the nonverbal key to a verbally comprehensible one in the mind of the therapist. This process is heightened for the therapist in the process of infant–parent psychotherapy, where the dyad's bidirectional communication of affect and intentionality is such a principal focus for the therapist.

The thesis of this paper is that a growing knowledge base has emerged about nonverbal behavior, as have formalized systems of classification, and that the infant–parent psychotherapist can make use of such systems to observe with greater discrimination. This applies to systems arising out of the Darwin-Ekman-Izard discrete-emotions tradition as well as out of the process-oriented intrinsic-meaning Laban-Kestenberg tradition. Other kinesic systems exist as well. While the formalized systems themselves may be useful for research, or in some cases inclusion in formalized assessment, the therapist trained in such a formalized system will likely see more meaningful expressions and their gradations in both infant and parent, and will be able to capture more about dyadic relatedness with greater precision.

Moreover, the KMP was introduced as a psychodynamically anchored system that provides the therapist with a language of movement and an enhanced eye for developmentally meaningful patterns and phrasing that go awry. Training in KMP notation and attainment of interrater reliability also work to enhance the accuracy of observations while helping clinical observers avoid attributional errors and more quickly gain awareness of countertransference issues.

By providing intrinsic connections between movement and meaning, the KMP offers a framework for developing impressions about the representational worlds of infant and parent, and about the particular affect realms (pleasure-displeasure, comfort-discomfort, or attraction-repulsion) in which reasonable degrees of harmony between infant and parent are not attained, or where they are most prone to derailment. The conjoint movement patterns of infant and parent can serve as entry points for the therapist, who can build on those patterns or clusters sufficiently demonstrating attunement in tension-flow (as a basis for empathic connectedness) and interactive adjustment in shape-flow (as a basis for reciprocal trust). The nonverbal dyadic exchange can lead the therapist to clinically attend to the impediments compromising sufficient understanding and predictability between partners. Methods of intervention can vary from the subjective/reflective/insight modality, informed by movement as to what conflicts or deficits are piqued, to more directive intervention which, through facilitated movement experience, makes more flexible and responsive the dyadic repertoire of collaborative patterns.

References

Ainsworth, M. D. S., Blehar, M. C., Waters, E., and Wall, S. (1978). *Patterns of Attachment: A Psychological Study of the Strange Situation.* Hillsdale, NJ: Erlbaum.

Alvarez, A., and Furgiuele, P. (1997). Speculations on components in the infant's sense of agency: the sense of abundance and the capacity to think in parentheses. In *Developments in Infant Observation: The Tavistock Model,* ed. S. Reid, pp. 123–139. London, UK: Routledge.

Amighi, J. K., Loman, S., Lewis, P., and Sossin, K. M. (1999). *The Meaning of Movement: Developmental and Clinical Perspectives of the Kestenberg Movement Profile.* Amsterdam: Gordon and Breach.

Bartenieff, I., and Lewis, D. (1980). *Body Movement: Coping with the Environment.* New York: Gordon and Breach.

Beebe, B. (1998). A procedural theory of therapeutic action: commentary on the symposium, "Interventions that Effect Change in Psychotherapy." *Infant Mental Health Journal* 19:333–340.

Beebe, B., Jaffe, J., Lachmann, F. L., et al. (2000). Systems models in development and psychoanalysis: the case of vocal rhythm coordination and attachment. *Infant Mental Health Journal* 21:99–122.

Beebe, B., and Lachmann, F. L. (1994). Representation and internalization in infancy: three principles of salience. *Pyschoanalytic Psychology* 11: 127–165.

——— (1998). Co-constructing inner and relational processes: self and mutual regulation in infant research and adult treatment. *Psychoanalytic Psychology* 15:1–37.

Beebe, B., Lachmann, F., and Jaffe, J. (1997). Mother–infant interaction structures and presymbolic self and object representations. *Psychoanalytic Dialogues* 7(2):133–182.

Bernstein, N. (1967). *Coordination and Regulation of Movements.* New York: Pergamon.

Berthoz, A. (2000). *The Brain's Sense of Movement.* Cambridge, MA: Harvard University Press.

Bick, E. (1964). Notes on infant observation in psychoanalytic training. *International Journal of Psycho-Analysis* 45:558–566.

Bowlby, J. (1988). *A Secure Base*. London, UK: Routledge.

Brazelton, T. B. (1992). *Touchpoints*. New York: Guilford.

Buelte, A. (1992). Movement retraining. In *The Body–Mind Connection in Human Movement Analysis*, ed. S. Loman and R. Brandt, pp. 109–118. Keene, NH: Antioch New England Graduate School.

Cohen, P., and Beebe, B. (in press). Video-feedback with a depressed mother and her infant: a collaborative, individual psychoanalytic and mother–infant treatment. *Journal of Infant, Child, and Adolescent Psychotherapy*.

Coll, X. (2000). Who needs to observe infants? Infant observation in the training of child and adolescent mental health workers. *Child Psychology and Psychiatry Review* 5:25–29.

Darwin, C. R. (1872). *The Expression of Emotions in Man and Animals*. Chicago: University of Chicago Press.

Davis, M. (1984). The state of the art: past and present trends in body movement research. In *Nonverbal Behavior: Applications and Cultural Implications*, ed. A. Wolfgang, pp. 203–228. New York: Academic Press.

Davis, M., and Hadicks, D. (1994). Nonverbal aspects of therapist attunement. *Journal of Clinical Psychology* 50:393–405.

Duke, M. P., and Nowicki, S. (1996). *Teach Your Child the Language of Social Success*. Atlanta: Peachtree Publishers.

Ekman, P., and Friesen, W. V. (1978). *Factial Action Coding System*. Palo Alto, CA: Consulting Psychologists Press.

Emde, R. N. (1993). Infant emotions and the caregiving environment. In *The IFEEL Pictures,* ed. R. N. Emde, J. Osofsky, and M. Butterfield, pp. 27–52. Madison, CT: International Universities Press.

Emde, R. N., Osofsky, J., and Butterfield, P. M., eds. (1993). *The IFEEL Pictures*. Madison, CT: International Universities Press.

Emde, R. N., and Sorce, J. F. (1983). The rewards of infancy: emotional availability and maternal referencing. In *Frontiers in Infant Psychiatry,* ed. J. D. Call, E. Galenson, and R. Tyson, pp. 17–30. New York: Basic Books.

Exner, J. E. (1993). *The Rorschach: A Comprehensive System: Vol. 1*. New York: Wiley.

Fonagy, P. (1994). Mental representations from an intergenerational cognitive science perspective. *Infant Mental Health Journal* 15:57–68.

Fraiberg, S. (1980). *Clinical Studies in Infant Mental Health*. New York: Basic Books.

Fraiberg, S., Adelson, E., and Shapiro, V. (1975). Ghosts in the nursery: a psychoanalytic approach to the problems of impaired infant–mother relationships. *Journal of the American Academy of Child Psychiatry* 14: 387–422.

Fridlund, A. J., Ekman, P., and Oster, H. (1987). Facial expressions of emotion. In *Nonverbal Behavior and Communication,* 2nd ed., ed. A. W. Siegman and S. Feldstein, pp. 143–223. Hillsdale, NJ: Erlbaum.

Galati, D., and Lavelli, M. (1997). Neonate and infant emotion expression perceived by adults. *Journal of Nonverbal Behavior* 21:57–83.

Gianino, A., and Tronick, E. Z. (1988). The mutual regulation model: the infant's self and interactive regulation, coping, and defense. In *Stress and coping,* ed. T. Field, P. McCabe, and N. Scheiderman, pp. 47–68. Hillsdale, NJ: Erlbaum.

Greenough, W. T., and Black, J. E. (1992). Induction of brain structure by experience: substrates for cognitive development. In *The Minnesota Symposia on Child Psychology: Vol. 24. Developmental Behavioral Neuroscience*, ed. M. R. Gunnar and C. A. Nelson, pp. 155–200. Hillsdale, NJ: Erlbaum.

Greenspan, S. I. (1997). *Developmentally Based Psychotherapy.* Madison, CT: International Universities Press.

Grice, P. (1989). *Studies in the Way of Words.* Cambridge, MA: Harvard University Press.

Hesse, E. (1999). The adult attachment interview: historical and current perspectives. In *Handbook of Attachment*, ed. J. Cassidy and P. R. Shaver, pp. 395–433. New York: Guilford.

Hirsbrunner, H. P., Frey, S., and Crawford, R. (1987). Movement in human interaction: description, parameter formation and analysis. In *Nonverbal Behavior and Communication*, 2nd ed., ed. A. W. Siegman and S. Feldstein, pp. 99–141. Hillsdale, NJ: Erlbaum.

Izard, C. E. (1979). *The Maximally Discriminative Facial Movement Coding System (MAX).* Newark, DE: University of Delaware, Instructional Resources Center.

——— (1982). Measuring emotions in human development. In *Measuring Emotions in Infants and Children.* Cambridge, UK: Cambridge University Press.

——— (1993). Organizational and motivational functions of discrete emotions. In *Handbook of Emotions*, ed. M. Lewis and J. M. Haviland, pp. 631–641. New York: Guilford.

Izard, C. E., and Dougherty, L. M. (1980). *System for Identifying Affect Expressions by Holistic Judgments (AFFEX)*. Newark, DE: University of Delaware, Instructional Resources Center.

Kestenberg, J. S. (1971). From organ-object imagery to self- and object-representations. In *Separation-Individuation: Papers in Honor of Margaret Mahler*, ed. J. B. McDevitt, pp. 75–99. New York: International Universities Press.

——— (1975). *Children and Parents*. New York: Aronson.

——— (1980). Pregnancy as a developmental phase. *Journal of Biological Experience* 3:58–66.

——— (1982). The inner-genital phase—prephallic and preoedipal. In *Early Female Development: Current Psychoanalytic Views*, ed. D. Mendell, pp. 81–125. Jamaica, NY: Spectrum.

——— (1985a). The flow of empathy and trust between mother and child. In *Parental Influences in Health and Disease*, ed. E. J. Anthony and G. H. Pollock, pp. 137–163. Boston: Little, Brown.

——— (1985b). The role of movement patterns in diagnosis and prevention. In *Paul Schilder: Mind Explorer*, ed. D. A. Shaskan and W. L. Roller, pp. 97–160. New York: Human Sciences.

——— (1987). Empathy for the fetus. In *Pre- and Perinatal Psychology: An Introduction*, ed. T. Verny, pp. 138–150. New York: Human Sciences.

——— (1990). What are the ingredients of bonding prenatally? *International Journal of Prenatal and Perinatal Studies* 1:119–124.

Kestenberg, J. S., and Borowitz, E. (1990). On narcissism and masochism in the fetus and the neonate. *Pre- and Perinatal Psychology Journal* 5: 87–94.

Kestenberg, J. S., and Buelte, A. (1977a). Prevention, infant therapy and the treatment of adults: 1. Toward understanding mutuality. *International Journal of Psychoanalytic Psychotherapy* 6:339–366.

——— (1977b). Prevention, infant therapy and the treatment of adults: 2. Mutual holding and holding-oneself-up. *International Journal of Psychoanalytic Psychotherapy* 6:369–396.

——— (1983). Prevention, infant therapy and the treatment of adults: 3. Periods of vulnerability in transitions from stability to mobility and vice versa. In *Frontiers of Infant Psychiatry*, ed. J. Call, E. Galenson, and R. Tyson, pp. 200–216. New York: Basic Books.

Kestenberg, J. S., Marcus, H., Sossin, K. M., and Stevenson, R. (1982). The development of paternal attitudes. In *Father and Child: Developmental and Clinical Perspectives*, ed. S. H. Cath, A. R. Gurwitt, and J. M. Ross, pp. 205–218. Boston: Little, Brown.

Kestenberg, J. S., and Sossin, K. M. (1979). *The Role of Movement Patterns in Development, II.* New York: Dance Notion Bureau.

Kestenberg, J. S., Sossin, K. M., Buelte, A., et al. (1993). Manifestations of aggression: an exploration of movement patterns. In *The Vulnerable Child, Vol. 1*, ed. T. B. Cohen, M. H. Etezady, and B. L. Pacella, pp. 67–87. Madison, CT: International Universities Press.

Laban, R. (1960). *The Mastery of Movement,* 2nd ed. London, UK: MacDonald & Evans.

——— (1966). *The Language of Movement: A Guidebook to Choreutics.* Boston: Plays.

Laban, R., and Lawrence, F. (1947). *Effort.* London: MacDonald & Evans.

La Barre, F. (2001). *On Moving and Being Moved: Nonverbal Behavior in Clinical Practice.* Hillsdale, NJ: Analytic Press.

Lewis, P. (1984). *Theoretical Approaches in Dance Movement Therapy.* Dubuque, IA: Kendall Hunt.

——— (1993). *Creative Transformation: The Healing Power of the Arts.* Wilmette, IL: Chiron.

——— (1999). Outline for the clinical interpretation of the Kestenberg Movement Profile with adults. In *The Meaning of Movement: Developmental and Clinical Perspectives of the Kestenberg Movement Profile*, ed. J. K. Amighi, S. Loman, P. Lewis, and K. M. Sossin, pp. 309–341. Amsterdam: Gordon and Breach.

Lieberman, A. F., Silverman, R., and Pawl, J. H. (2000). Infant–parent psychotherapy: core concepts and current approaches. In *Handbook of Infant Mental Health*, 2nd ed., ed. C. H. Zeanah, Jr., pp. 472–484. New York: Guilford.

Lieberman, A. F., and Zeanah, C. H. (1999). Contributions of attachment theory to infant–parent psychotherapy and other interventions with infants and young children. In *Handbook of Attachment: Theory, Research and Clinical Applications*, ed. J. Cassidy and P. R. Shaver, pp. 555–574. New York: Guilford.

Loman, S. (1994). Attuning to the fetus and the young child: approaches from dance movement therapy. *Zero To Three* 15:20–26.

——— (1995). The case of Warren: a KMP approach to autism. In *Dance and Other Expressive Art Therapies: When Words Are Not Enough*, ed. F. Levy, pp. 213–223. New York: Routledge Publications.

Loman, S., and Merman, H. (1996). The KMP: a tool for dance/movement therapy. *American Journal of Dance Therapy* 18:29–51.

Lyons-Ruth, K., and Jacobvitz, D. (1999). Attachment disorganization: unresolved loss, relational violence and lapses in behavioral and attentional strategies. In *Handbook of Attachment: Theory, Research and Clinical Applications*, ed. J. Cassidy and P. R. Shaver, pp. 520–554. New York: Guilford.

Main, M. (1991). Metacognitive knowledge, metacognitive monitoring, and singular (coherent) vs. multiple (incoherent) models of attachment: findings and directions for future research. In *Attachment Across the Life Cycle*, ed. C. M. Parkes, J. Stevenson-Hinde, and P. Marris, pp. 127–159. London, UK: Routledge.

Main, M., Kaplan, N., and Cassidy, J. (1985). Security in infancy, childhood and adulthood: a move to the level of representation. In *Growing Points of Attachment Theory and Research*, ed. I. Bretherton, and E. Waters, *Monographs of the Society for Research in Child Development* 50(1–2, Serial No. 209), 66–104.

Main, M., and Solomon, J. (1990). Procedures for identifying infants as disorganized/disoriented during the Ainsworth strange situation. In *Attachment in the Preschool Years: Theory, Research and Intervention*, ed. M. T. Greenberg, D. Cicchetti, and E. M. Cummings, pp. 121–160. Chicago: University of Chicago Press.

McDonough, S. C. (1993). Interaction guidance: understanding and treating early infant–caregiver relationship disorders. In *Handbook of Infant Mental Health*, ed. C. H. Zeanah, Jr., pp. 414–426. New York: Guilford.

Miller, L., Rustin, M., and Shuttleworth, J., eds. (1989). *Closely Observed Infants*. London, UK: Duckworth.

Nelson, C. A. (2000). The neurobiological bases of early intervention. In *Handbook of Early Childhood Intervention*, 2nd ed., ed. J. P. Shonkoff and S. J. Meisels, pp. 204–227. Cambridge, UK: Cambridge University Press.

Oster, H., Alfiere, T., and Taufique, S. (1997). *The effects of craniofacial anomalies on infant facial expression and maternal psychological adjustment*. Presentation at Institute of Psychology Conference, University of Salzburg, Austria, July 18.

Prince, R. (2001). Editor's introduction: Kestenberg paper. *Section V: Continuing Professional Education Program*. Turning Point Series. APA, Division 39, Section V, Psychonanlytic Clinicians. [Online: http://www.divpsa.org/div39/section5/ceuprogam/kestenberg/editorsnote.html]

Reid, S. (1997). Introduction: psychoanalytic infant observation. In *Developments in Infant Observation: The Tavistock Model*. London, UK: Routledge.

Romer, G., and Sossin, K. M. (1990). Parent–infant holding patterns and their impact on infant perceptual and interactional experience. *Pre- and Peri-Natal Psychology* 5:69–85.

Rourke, B., ed. (1989). *Syndrome of Nonverbal Learning Disabilities: Neurodevelopmental Manifestations*. New York: Guilford.

Russell, R. C., Grignon, M., and Royer, J. (1995). Infant observation: a relevant educational method for psychiatrists and other mental health practitioners. *Infant Psychiatry* 4:529–538.

Sandler, J., and Sandler, A. M. (1978). On the development of object relationships and affects. *International Journal of Psycho-Analysis* 59:285–296.

Schilder, P. (1935). *The Image and Appearance of the Human Body*. London, UK: Kegan Paul, French, Trubner.

Schore, A. (1997). Interdisciplinary developmental research as a source of clinical models. In *The Neurobiological and Developmental Basis for Psychotherapeutic Intervention*, ed. M. Moskowitz, C. Monk, C. Kaye, and S. Ellman, pp. 1–71. Northvale, NJ: Aronson.

Seligman, S. (2000). Clinical interviews with families of infants. In *Handbook of Infant Mental Health*, 2nd ed., ed. C. H. Zeanah, Jr., pp. 211–221. New York: Guilford.

Solomon, J., and George, C. (1999). The measurement of attachment security in infancy and childhood. In *Handbook of Attachment: Theory, Research and Clinical Applications*, ed. J. Cassidy and P. R. Shaver, pp. 287–317. New York: Guilford.

Sossin, K. M. (1993). Pre- and postnatal repercussions of handicapping conditions upon the narcissistic line of development. *Pre- and Perinatal Psychology Journal* 7(3):195–213.

——— (1999a). The KMP and infant–parent psychotherapy. In *The Meaning of Movement: Developmental and Clinical Perspectives of the Kestenberg Movement Profile*, ed. J. K. Amighi, S. Loman, P. Lewis, and K. M. Sossin, pp. 191–209. Amsterdam: Gordon and Breach.

——— (1999b). Interpretation of an adult profile: observations in a parent–child setting. In *The Meaning of Movement: Developmental and Clinical Perspectives of the Kestenberg Movement Profile*, ed. J. K. Amighi, S. Loman, P. Lewis, and K. M. Sossin, pp. 265–290. Amsterdam: Gordon and Breach.

Sossin, K. M., and Loman, S. (1992). Clinical applications of the KMP. In *The Body–Mind Connection in Human Movement Analysis*, ed. S. Loman, pp. 21–55. Keene, NH: Antioch New England Graduate School.

Stern, D. N. (1985). *The Interpersonal World of the Infant.* New York: Basic Books.

——— (1995). *The Motherhood Constellation: A Unified View of Parent–Infant Psychotherapy.* New York: Basic Books.

Szajnberg, N. M. (1993). The IFEEL Pictures as a projective instrument: pre- and full-term mothers. In *The IFEEL Pictures*, ed. R. N. Emde, J. Osofsky, and P. M. Butterfield, pp. 207–216. Madison, CT: International Universities Press.

Termine, N. T., and Izard, C. E. (1988). Infants' responses to their mothers' expressions of joy and sadness. *Developmental Psychology* 24:223–229.

Tomkins, S. (1962). *Affect, Imagery, Consciousness, Vol. 1: The Positive Affects.* New York: Springer.

Tortora, S. (1994). Join my dance: the unique movement style of each infant and toddler can invite communication, expression and intervention. *Zero to Three* 15:1–10.

Tronick, E. Z. (1998). Dyadically expanded states of consciousness and the process of therapeutic change. *Infant Mental Health Journal* 19: 290–299.

Tronick, E. Z., and Cohn, J. (1989). Infant–mother face-to-face interaction: age and gender differences in coordination and the occurrence of miscoordinations. *Child Development* 60:85–91.

van Ijzendoorn, M. H. (1995). Adult attachment representations, parental responsiveness, and infant attachment: a meta-analysis on the predictive validity of the Adult Attachment Interview. *Psychological Bulletin* 117: 387–403.

Wittenberg, I. (1997). Beginnings: the family, the observer and the infant observation group. In *Developments in Infant Observation: The Tavistock Model*, ed. S. Reid, pp. 19–32. London, UK: Routledge.

Zeanah, C. H., Jr., and Boris, N. W. (2000). Disturbances and disorders of attachment in early childhood. In *Handbook of Infant Mental Health*, 2nd ed., ed. C. H. Zeanah, Jr., pp. 353–368. New York: Guilford.

Zelenko, M., and Benham, A. (2000). Videotaping as a therapeutic tool in psychodynamic infant–parent therapy. *Infant Mental Health Journal* 21: 192–203.

BOOK REVIEW

CLINICAL AND OBSERVATIONAL PSYCHOANALYTIC RESEARCH: ROOTS OF A CONTROVERSY BY ANDRÉ GREEN AND DANIEL STERN

Reviewed by Phyllis Ackman, Ph.D.

This book is based on a very stormy meeting held at University College, London, on November 1, 1997, between André Green and Daniel Stern, under the chairmanship of Joseph Sandler. Several discussants, including Anne Alvarez, Rosine Perelberg, and Irma Brenman Pick, comment on the two main position papers, with further replies by the main speakers.

Ricardo Steiner, in his thoroughgoing introduction, informs us that the wish to discuss the pros and cons of what Freud called "the cooperation of the two methods," that is, the clinical method and the research method, was the main reason that lay behind organizing such a meeting. The edited proceedings of that conference are reproduced in Part II of the monograph; a preliminary debate, which was first published in the *International Psychoanalytical Association Newsletter*, is presented in Part I.

Due to his death in October 1998, Joseph Sandler never completed this monograph on the debate over the role of infant research and all empirical research to psychoanalysis. The book is dedicated to Sandler as a fitting completion of the work he had begun.

The two points of view represented in the debate are very different ways of understanding and interpreting psychoanalysis as well as what it means to be a psychoanalyst today. They bring into strong focus the issues of how to evaluate and use empirical research, including infant observation research, in the psychoanalytic endeavor.

Steiner spells out vividly the differences in the two points of view. André Green defends Freud's clinical and metapsychological views, particularly the drive theory. The superordinate concept for him is that of "après coup," Freud's "nachtraglichkeit" or deferred action. This theoretical notion does not allow for any event experienced in the life of the infant to be considered the legitimate province of psychoanalysis. Only those events that can be reconstructed post facto, with all the distortions, condensations, and other hallmarks of the primary process and unconscious defenses, constitute the true material for psychoanalysis. This viewpoint is at the core of Green's disagreement with Stern and other infant researchers such as Emde and Fonagy. Stern's major emphasis, on the other hand, is on the lived experience of the infant in the here and now. Stern studies the preverbal interactions, body movements, and affect-laden, observable, aconflictual communications between mother and baby. These comprise the lived experience for the baby. He attempts to take the point of view of the baby in the "coup," or the action in the present.

A major dichotomy exists between Green's definition of psychoanalysis as "intrapsychic," with its model of psychic reality based on unconscious conflicts, the dream, and its processes, and Stern's notion of "observable interaction" between infant and mother, as being a legitimate part of psychoanalysis. Green defends the clinical setting as the only place where rigorous psychoanalysis can get its knowledge, not about the infant but about the infantile. The real infant does not figure in any important way as far as he is concerned. The infantile in the adult patient is reachable only through free associations and interpretations of the patient and the analyst.

Green becomes polemical about research, calling it science fiction. He can see no value, heuristic or otherwise, in empirically based developmental research. He sees it as "dangerous" because it can destroy the "specificity" of psychoanalysis. Steiner points out in the introduction that it is not by chance that infant observation forms no part of the training curriculum in either of the French psychoanalytic societies belonging to the IPA.

The first part of the monograph includes an exchange of views between Green and Robert Wallerstein, a pioneer in empirical research in psychoanalysis. This discussion on the relevance of empirical research for psychoanalysis is published in the *IPA Newsletter* of 1997. In this essay Green expresses grave concern that research will lead to the oversimplification of psychoanalytic knowledge. He is full of praise for certain psychoanalysts, who, with their knowledge from the single mode of working with their patients, have come up with dazzling insights. Green believes that Stern's research can be of interest for psychological knowledge, but is of little help for psychoanalytic theory. For Green there is an apparent dichotomy between psychological data based on empirical findings and psychoanalytic theory. The implications of this point of view are very serious for those of us in psychoanalysis who consider our work consistent with contemporary science. By Green's definition, concepts like *the stimulus barrier* should still be part of psychoanalytic theory, even though we have ample empirical evidence that contradicts it. We have been provided with information on how from the earliest days an infant cuts down on stimulation that is overwhelming by gaze aversion at first. This excellent work on self and mutual regulation patterns has had an enormous impact on the way we think of the infant and his capacities particularly in the realm of mother and infant interaction (Beebe et al. 1997). For Green, theory as it once was is sacrosanct and impermeable to new evidence.

Green recognizes that it is interesting to observe the development of the infant more closely and carefully, but believes that psychological development should not be confused with the psychoanalytic endeavor, which can be done only in the consulting room, using the model of the mind that he endorses. The door gets slammed shut. He disputes the psychoanalytic training of the researchers who are also psychoanalysts calling them "screen trainings." What has to be kept alive is the specific mental state that inhabits the psychoanalyst during his work. He obviously feels that research does nothing for that and he hints at even more insidious effects.

Wallerstein, of course, disagrees and makes it clear that it is "dauntingly difficult to do research that is simultaneously faithful both to the highly subjective and complex data of the consulting room and to the objective concerns of the empirical scientific inquiry." He states that science is not defined by its content but by its method of inquiry, and the challenge is to accomplish its necessary work by methods that do not violate the "spirit" of the domain studied. He also disagrees about the arbitrary separation between psychology and psychoanalysis, saying that integrating rather than separating the two is the direction we must follow.

Green is in complete agreement with Peter Wolff (1996). Wolff shares his rigid adherence to earlier Freudian models of the mind. Green scrutinized the list of references in the published papers of both Stern and Emde, as well as those who participated in the Wolff debate, and counted the "non-psychoanalytic" papers, concluding that for the most part the authors quoted are openly opposed to psychoanalysis. The obvious fact that these researchers are attempting to build bridges between the developmentalists and psychoanalysts and that this is why they have references to the published papers in developmental journals escapes Green (Emde and Fonagy 1997, Fonagy 1996). He sees these references as proof of their opposition to psychoanalysis.

When information and empirical evidence are of no value unless the basic motivations and assumptions of the authors are critically assessed, we are caught in an *ad hominem* issue of control over ideas. Green goes on to say that what an analyst thinks outside of the consulting room will significantly affect what he thinks when doing analysis. His basic belief harks back to the Freud statement that the therapeutic influence of psychoanalysis depends on the replacement of unconscious mental acts by conscious ones (Freud 1926). Other points of view that have entered psychoanalysis are seen as attempts to destroy psychoanalysis (Gabbard 1995).

According to Green, the dream is the basic paradigm and the lived experience of the child is not the material of psychoanalysis. It is the dream of the lived experience that counts. Only then do we have the "après coup," what has been important during the previous day that escaped our attention, a fantasy that has been repressed, sorted out through the dreamwork onto latent thoughts. Only then does the analyst know what has really been important from the point of view of the unconscious. Templates of the past unconscious are internal structures that orient later experiences. We carry within ourselves the totality of our past not as memories but as a set of organizers. How as analysts can we disagree with this last formulation? What Green prefers not to see is that these templates are exactly what Stern is talking about as the lived experience that becomes represented and continues to develop into preverbal, implicit, procedural knowing.

Needless to say, Green holds Bowlby responsible as the chief troublemaker and the initiator of the scientific movement that is diminishing psychoanalysis.

Stern responds by taking up the issue of relevance. His argument is essentially based on philosophy of science tenets (Ricoeur 1997). He agrees with Green that infant observation can never prove or disprove a clinical tenet of psychoanalysis. He turns to what he thinks is a more important question: Can infant observation be indirectly relevant to psychoanalysis? Ultimately the way psychoanalysis is viewed by the broader world, including the scientific world, rests on its plausibility. For example, the "normal" autistic phase is simply not plausible in light of the findings of infant observation. This research does not disprove the existence of such a phase; however it does act to isolate this psychoanalytic tenet from the mainstream of general knowledge that further makes its acceptability precarious to the larger scholarly and scientific world.

In response to Green's polemical attack that infant research is pseudoscience, Stern argues that there are many modes of science. They can't all be clumped together and dismissed as one. The most pertinent mode for Stern is hypothesis generating as against hypothesis testing. This distinction is critical. The wide-ranging reflection and exposure to all kinds of human experiences must necessarily precede quantitative research, where the aim is to generate hypotheses, not to test them.

As has been mentioned, Stern is interested in the currently lived experiences of the infant from the infant's perspective. It is this lived experience that lays down memory traces and is what is represented. He raises the question of how experience can get structured in the very present moment of its being lived, suggesting that form and sense are imposed during the experience itself. The young infant does not need a verbal symbolic process to form, make sense of, or even revise his immediate raw experience as it is happening. We have much evidence from research to support these early capacities of infants.

The thrust of Stern's argument is that infancy researchers and psychoanalysts have much to tell each other, neither to confirm nor reject notions within each other's domain, but to stimulate, inspire, and provide a wider knowledge base.

The discussants, Rosine Perelberg, Anne Alvarez, and Irma Brenman Pick, cast their votes between the two major points of view, but in general make it clear that their adult work has been enriched by the infant research studies of Trevarthan, the maternal depression research by Lynn Murray, and so on. They speak of enriched understanding that promotes cross-fertilization. Alvarez particularly takes issue with the model that Green adheres to, finding that in her work with profoundly disturbed children she requires a different paradigm that relies heavily on an excellent grasp of early development. She goes on to illustrate how Stern's work on vitality affects have added a greater clarity to some of Bion's concepts.

Discussions from the floor end the meeting with some trenchant comments by David Tuckett about the difficulty of giving up old ideas in psychoanalysis, sometimes overvaluing them to extreme degrees.

In reading this deeply polemical discussion I found myself wondering what Freud's participation might have been. While one can select from early or later papers confirmation for one's point of view, the genius of Freud lay in what is certainly implicit in all the writings—that psychoanalysis is a work in progress. The blueprint for each person must remain incomplete. I am convinced that he would have been deeply excited by current work in the brain behavior area, in dynamic systems theory, and in these deeply interesting developmental studies that promise to shed light on those early templates that become the essential patterns of later experience. Surely Freud would have been struck by the peculiar property of development we are beginning to recognize now, its complex and unpredictable patterning that is increasingly understood as non-linear, epigenetic, and recently even chaotic. Aren't we capable as analysts of keeping these thoughts in the background as we listen to our patients? Shouldn't this openness and curiosity be the essential ingredient in our training of psychoanalysts?

References

Beebe, B., Lachmann, F., and Jaffe, J. (1997). Mother–infant interaction structures and presymbolic self and object representations. *Psychoanalytic Dialogues* 7(2):133–182.

Emde, R. N., and Fonagy, P. (1997). Guest editorial: An emerging culture for psychoanalytic research? *International Journal of Psycho-Analysis* 78:115–134.

Fonagy, P. (1996). Discussion of Peter Wolff's paper, "Infant Observation and Psychoanalysis." *Journal of the American Psychoanalytic Association* 44(2):404–422.

Freud, S. (1926 [1925]). Psychoanalysis. *Standard Edition* 20:259–270.

Gabbard, G. (1995). The emerging common ground. *International Journal of Psycho-Analysis* 76:475–486.

Ricoeur, P. (1997). The question of proof in Freud's psychoanalytic writings. *Journal of the American Psychoanalytic Association* 25:835–871.

Wolff, P. (1996). The irrelevance of infant observation for psychoanalysis. *Journal of the American Psychoanalytic Association* 44:369–473.

Preparation. Manuscripts submitted for publication should be well organized and have a narrative of no more than 25 pages of double-spaced text in 12-point font. Typed or printed on 8½-by-11-inch paper, they must have 1-inch margins on all sides to allow for editorial remarks. They should be prepared in accordance with the *Publication Manual of the American Psychological Association* (4th ed.). Comments should be submitted no later than the following quarterly issue and should be limited to about five pages. A separate cover sheet must provide the author's full name, address, telephone, fax, and e-mail address, if available.

Review Policy. Following a preliminary review by the Editor, manuscripts will be reviewed by the Editorial Board. Selection of manuscripts for publication is based on blind peer review. Therefore, each copy of the manuscript should include a separate title page with the author's name and affiliations.

Disk Preparation. The author will supply an electronic version of his or her manuscript on disk. It should preferably be IBM-compatible in either Word or WordPerfect on a 3.5-inch diskette. It should be prepared accurately and simply, avoiding the use of elaborate formatting or special fonts. Paragraphs should be formatted the same way throughout. The disk must be labeled with the author's name, title of the manuscript, and hardware and software used.

Manuscript Submission. Four copies of the manuscript or comment should be submitted, and all copies should be clean and on paper of good quality. Mail manuscripts to Kirkland Vaughans, Editor, 66 Lincoln Avenue, Wyandanch, NY 11798. Be sure to retain a copy for your files. Manuscripts will be acknowledged upon receipt.